ACHIEVING IMPACT IN PUBLIC SERVICE

Essays in honour of Sylda Langford

Edited by

Donal de Buitleir

INSTITUTE OF PUBLIC
ADMINISTRATION

First published in 2021
by the Institute of Public Administration
57-61 Lansdowne Road
Dublin 4
www.ipa.ie

British Library cataloguing-in-publication data
A catalogue record for this book is available from
the British Library

ISBN: 978-1-910393-38-3

Cover design by Signal Design, Dublin
Typeset by Carole Lynch, Sligo
Printed by Colorman, Dublin

CONTENTS

PART III: The Citizen and the State
– Policy, Governance and Engagement

ACKNOWLEDGEMENTS

I would like to thank the authors who responded so generously to the invitation to contribute to this volume. I am also very grateful to Anne Vaughan, Ita Mangan, Patricia O'Hara and Leonie Lunny who proposed this publication and invited me to be its Editor. Special thanks are also due to Emer Ryan and Carolyn Gormley of the Institute of Public Administration for their help in preparing this volume for publication.

DONAL DE BUITLEIR

NOTES ON THE AUTHORS

Delma Byrne is Associate Professor at Maynooth University Department of Sociology. The primary focus of her work is around social stratification in education, the graduate labour market and the effects of child poverty. Her research uses both qualitative and quantitative approaches, and longitudinal data to examine these issues. Her work spans academic research and publications, but also has a clear applied focus, conducting research for public and voluntary bodies and statistical analyses of public administrative datasets.

Donal de Buitleir is Chairman of the Professional Standards Board of Chartered Accountants Ireland and a member of the Policing Authority. He spent the early part of his career in the civil service, ending up as Assistant Secretary in the Office of the Revenue Commissioners. He worked for 20 years in the private sector (AIB Group). Since leaving the civil service, he has chaired or been a member of Government Review bodies in the areas of local government, health, education and taxation and welfare policy. He is an Eisenhower Fellow.

Josephine Feehily was a career civil servant, principally in the Department of Social Welfare and the Office of the Revenue Commissioners, from where she retired as Chairman. She established and was the first Chair of the Policing Authority and chaired the Commission on Pensions. She was raised in her family's pub, first in Limerick city and later County Limerick.

Sinéad Hanafin worked as the Head of Research at the Department of Health and Children/Children and Youth Affairs from 2003 to 2011, during which time she led the development and implementation of the national children's research programme. Prior to that, she worked as a nurse, midwife, public health nurse and lecturer at UCC and the RCSI. She holds an MSc from Trinity College Dublin, PhD from King's College London and Fellowship (Ad Eundem) from the RCSI. She is a scholar of the European Academy of Nursing Science and is widely published nationally and internationally in areas relating to children's lives, strategic data and research development and public health nursing. She is currently a Visiting Research Fellow at

Trinity College Dublin and the Managing Director of Research Matters (www.researchmatters.eu).

Nóirín Hayes is a Visiting Academic at the School of Education, Trinity College Dublin and Professor Emerita, Technological University Dublin. Working within a bio-ecological framework of development and through a child rights lens, she researches in early childhood education and care (ECEC) with a particular focus on early learning, curriculum and pedagogy, and ECEC policy. She is convener of the Researching Early Childhood Education Collaborative (RECEC) at Trinity College and has authored many reports, articles and books. She is co-author of *Introducing Bronfenbrenner: A Guide* (Routledge, 2017), *In Search of Social Justice: John Bennett's Lifetime Contribution to Early Childhood Policy and Practice* (Routledge, 2018) and *Supporting Positive Behaviour in Early Childhood Settings and Primary Schools: Relationships, Reciprocity and Reflection* (Routledge, 2020). She is a founder member of the Children's Rights Alliance and an Honorary Member of OMEP International.

Ursula Kilkelly is Professor of Law at the School of Law, University College Cork. Ursula has worked for 25 years in the area of international children's rights and youth justice, undertaking original research and publishing nearly 100 articles and books across these areas nationally and internationally. Ursula's work promotes the implementation of children's rights into law, policy and practice, and she is strongly committed to improving the lives of children through a variety of evidence-based approaches. Evident of this commitment to putting research into practice, Ursula has been Chairperson of the Board of Management of Oberstown Children Detention Campus, the national facility for the care of children detained by the courts, where she has led the organisation through a period of extraordinary reform and change. Ursula was reappointed to this role in 2019 by the Minister for Children and Youth Affairs.

Leonie Lunny retired as Chief Executive of the Citizens Information Board in 2008, having worked there for 20 years. Prior to 1988, she had worked for 14 years as a Senior Social Worker in the Community Care Programme in the Eastern Health Board, with responsibility for Family Support Services and Child Protection. Throughout the years, she has participated in a range of working groups and initiatives, including the Monageer Inquiry and the Roscommon Inquiry.

Dermot McCarthy is a former Secretary-General to the Government and Secretary-General to the Department of the Taoiseach. Since retiring in 2011, he has been active on a voluntary basis in a number of non-profit organisations, principally engaged in social care and education, as well as serving as a permanent deacon in the Archdiocese of Dublin.

Ita Mangan is a barrister who has specialised in welfare and citizens' rights. She has had extensive involvement in public inquiries. She was Chair of the Citizens Information Board from 2015 to 2020 and is currently a member of the AIB Tracker Appeals Panel, Chair of Age and Opportunity and a board member of the Irish Hospice Foundation.

Eddie Molloy is an independent management consultant. He was an outside member of the Mullarkey Group that updated the system of accountability of accounting officers and secretaries general in 2002 and he has been engaged since then in a number of consultations on public service accountability. He has carried out assignments in most government departments and numerous public service agencies, including the Revenue Commissioners, the Office of the Comptroller and Auditor General, the HSE and An Garda Síochána.

Mary Murphy is Professor in the Department of Sociology, Maynooth University, with research interests in gender and social security, globalisation and welfare states, and power and civil society. She co-edited *The Irish Welfare State in the 21st Century: Challenges and Changes* (Palgrave, 2016) and *Policy Analysis in Ireland* (Policy Press, 2021). An active advocate for social justice and gender equality, she is a member of the Council of State.

Patricia O'Hara is a sociologist who has held positions in research, teaching, and policy analysis, and has published widely. She has been Chair and member of various boards and advisory committees to Government. Prior to her retirement in 2019, she was Chairperson of the National Statistics Board, a member of the European Statistical Governance Advisory Board (ESGAB) and Adjunct Professor at Maynooth University. She has also served on the boards of NGOs, including as Chair of Jigsaw, the national centre for youth mental health, until 2020. She was educated at UCC, University of South Carolina and TCD where she was awarded a PhD.

Emily O'Reilly served as Ireland's national, public service Ombudsman from 2003 to 2013. Since October 2013, she has been serving as European

Ombudsman, dealing with complaints against the institutions of the European Union.

Cormac Quinlan is Director of Transformation and Policy in Tusla. Cormac is a registered social worker and has worked since 1997 in the area of child protection and welfare. In addition to being a tutor with the Master in Social Work Programme in TCD for many years, he has also held the position of both Chair and a member of the Social Work Registration Board. A main area of interest for Cormac throughout his career has been practice development in the area of child protection, welfare and family support. As Director of Transformation and Policy, Cormac holds lead responsibility for national adoption services, policy and research, the project management office, and strategy and business planning. Since joining Tusla's national office, Cormac has led a number of strategic programmes including the Child Protection and Welfare Strategy, which is aimed at implementing a national approach to practice across child protection and welfare services.

Anne Vaughan was Deputy Secretary in the then Department of Employment Affairs and Social Protection for almost eight years, where she had responsibility for policy development and service delivery in relation to working-age payments. She retired in 2018. She has a special interest in pensions policy and was a member of The Pensions Authority and the Pensions Commission. She is currently Chairperson of the National Statistics Board and a member of the Commission on Taxation and Welfare. Other activities include mentoring and coaching, and membership of a number of not-for-profit boards.

INTRODUCTION

Why this book?

This book is inspired by the long and distinguished career of Sylda Langford, considered by many to be one of the most outstanding public servants of her generation. Sylda's work across social work and social policy involved addressing problems and formulating and implementing solutions to some of the most serious challenges facing any society – those concerned with children and our most vulnerable people. In her ascent through the civil service, her work was distinguished by a penetrating analysis and understanding of issues, often based on her direct experiences of service delivery and policy implementation prior to becoming a civil servant.

To celebrate Sylda's contribution to Irish life over many years, we invited a distinguished group of authors to contribute essays covering the main areas of her work. Given her commitment to finding innovative solutions and promoting change to improve the lives of some of the most vulnerable and disadvantaged in our society, we asked authors to make their essays forward-looking, while taking due account of past and current developments.

Sylda Langford's public life – a brief history

Sylda (Hayes) was born and grew up in the small town of Doon, Co. Limerick, where her parents had a pub and a farm. The eldest of four children, she was fortunate enough to live within walking distance of a girls' secondary school in the days before free secondary education and school transport. She did well at school but her parents, realising that life in a busy home behind a pub might affect her schoolwork, enrolled her as a boarder for her final two years in secondary school. Her schooling, experience of pub and farm life, and small-town living in post-war rural Ireland were among influences on her lifelong concern with social progress and justice.

In the early 1970s, having graduated from University College Cork with first class Bachelor's and Master's degrees, Sylda spent three years in Brazil, developing social services in poverty-stricken communities while also lecturing on community development. Her experiences of working on the ground as a social worker strengthened her conviction of the value and effectiveness of the community development approach in addressing inequality and disadvantage. Some of the projects she set up in Brazil became models of practice that were later widely replicated there.

On returning to Ireland, she began her career as a development officer with the National Social Service Council (now the Citizens Information Board), supporting social service councils and local service provision. There, using a community development approach, she was instrumental in setting up groups that evolved into local development organisations. In 1976/7, Sylda took leave from the Council to attend the London School of Economics (LSE), where she received her Certificate of Qualification in Social Work (CQSW) with Distinction.

After returning to Ireland, she married Shay Langford, the love of her life. Shay's sudden and untimely death in 1999 was an almost unbearable loss for Sylda and their four children.

In 1980, she became a social worker with the Eastern Health Board in Wicklow where her role included providing family support and child protection services. There, when providing support services in the community or placing children in foster or residential care, she saw at first hand the interface between state services and children and families 'at risk'. She was also involved with adoption services and the development and support of facilities such as day centres and crèches. While in Wicklow, Sylda co-founded the voluntary organisation then called Parents Under Stress (now Parentline).

Leaving Wicklow as Senior Social Worker in 1985, Sylda became an investigator in the Office of the Ombudsman, one of the first non-civil servants to do so. While there, she pioneered the practice of holding public consultations in local centres with social service and community development organisations. She was instrumental in focusing the office on individual rights and holding public bodies to account, and she became thoroughly familiar with the range of issues surrounding the relationship between the citizen and the state.

In the early 1990s, Sylda was successful in the then Department of Social Welfare's competition for Principal Officer. This was a strategic move – she was keenly aware that by working inside the 'system' she could help effect the kind of changes her work in communities had shown her were necessary. As a Principal, she worked on issues related to poverty, community development and the community and voluntary sector. She oversaw a reappraisal of the supplementary welfare allowance scheme; the computerisation of data for that scheme; the role of rent supplement as a housing aid; and the implementation of grants for community and local development under the EU Structural Funds arrangements.

By the late 1990s, Sylda had advanced to become Assistant Secretary in the then Department of Justice, Equality and Law Reform (DJELR), with responsibility for the equality agenda. This level of seniority gave her an opportunity to lead on a range of equality issues. In particular, she promoted a 'whole of government' approach to these matters and tried to ensure that all relevant departments were involved. She was deeply involved in implementing the policy decision to mainstream services for people with disabilities. In 2000, this led to, among other things, the transfer of training and employment services for people with disabilities from the then National Rehabilitation Board (NRB) to Foras Áiseanna Saothar (FÁS), the transfer of other NRB services to Comhairle (the renamed National Social Service Council, which has since been renamed the Citizens Information Board), and the establishment of the National Disability Authority. In 2005, the Disability Act provided for the assessment of need for people with disabilities. Other departments, particularly the Departments of Education and Health, were also introducing new provisions for people with disabilities. Sylda was also involved in the development of the Employment Equality Act, 1998 and the Equal Status Act, 2000.

The equality agenda and access to significant EU funding for gender equality programmes provided an opportunity for a ground-breaking initiative in the form of the Equal Opportunities Childcare Programme (EOCP). Sylda's unique role in this was to recognise the substantial importance of childcare as a policy focus and to maximise the potential of the opportunities presented for the broader agenda of Early Childhood Care and Education (ECCE). The challenges were many, including the fact that at least six departments were involved to some degree in the support, funding or regulation of childcare. A national programme to support childcare was unprecedented in Ireland, and bringing it to the policy table involved overcoming considerable scepticism and resistance within the system. However, Sylda persisted, and the resulting programme, based on a community model organised on a county basis, has evolved into a substantial and well-respected national service.

She established a Childcare Directorate within the DJELR and moved to develop a National Childcare Strategy which would integrate the different strands of policy arrangements for childcare and early educational services. It was clear that it made sense to create a structure that would, in her words, be 'child-centred' and integrate the areas of childcare, child protection, children's rights and services and juvenile justice. The Office of the Minister for Children was established in 2005, with Sylda as Director General. This later became the Office for Children and Youth Affairs and, in 2011, a full government department. It was renamed in 2020 as the Department of Children, Equality, Disability, Integration and Youth.

As is evident from the contributions that follow, Sylda's influence has been far-reaching in many fields – from promoting the basic principle that good evidence makes good policy, to initiating and steering substantial advances in equality, child and youth policy, and having a seminal influence on services for children. There is now a clear awareness of the unique nature and importance of the ECCE sector and a structure in place that has grown incrementally and provides much-needed services to families.

Sylda was also a leader and influencer in more low-key ways across a range of policy areas. She understood the strategic value of philanthropic funding earlier than most and responded thoughtfully to proposals that could support children, young people and marginalised communities. The significant investment of such funds in early childhood, youth mental health and intellectual disability initiatives, and in the promotion of better services, is due in no small part to her influence and support.

Following her retirement in 2010, she continued her commitment to public service. She acted as Chair of boards and review groups, including the Citizens Information Board, 2010–15; the Review of Domiciliary Care Allowance, 2012; the Mobility Allowance and Motorised Transport Review Group, 2013; and the National Maternity Strategy Group, 2015–16. She was a non-executive board director of the HSE; the Child and Family Agency (TUSLA); Oberstown Children Detention Campus; and Limerick Regeneration. She was also a member of the Ryan Report Monitoring Group and the Homeless Oversight Group. Sylda was a board member of We the Citizens, which promoted the concept of Citizens' Assemblies. In addition, she was always, and continues to be, generous with her time, providing advice and mentoring to the many people in the civil and public service who seek her guidance.

Book structure

This book is structured around the key themes of Sylda's working life – her contribution to developing evidence-based policies and services to improve the lives of children and address social exclusion. Her work on the welfare of children and young people has been seminal and she was the key architect of the structures and systems underpinning childcare policy, juvenile justice, adoption, child protection and equal status that exist today.

Part I: Putting Practice into Policy – Understanding the Needs of Children

Part I takes up Sylda's focus on children's needs and the importance of underpinning policy with facts and marshalling evidence. She understood that what is counted is what matters and that robust data underpin the measurement of progress. In this context, a key initiative during her time as Director General of the Office of the Minister for Children was funding of the National Longitudinal Study of Children – *Growing Up in Ireland*. This is one of the largest and most complex studies of this nature that has ever been undertaken in Ireland, tracking the development of two cohorts of young children (18,000 in total) since its initiation in 2006. Its actual and potential contribution to our understanding of children and young people's lives is immense.

The first two chapters, by Delma Byrne and Sinéad Hanafin, draw on, and explain the origin of, the substantial body of information and research on children that Sylda spearheaded. Byrne reviews recent trends in the prevalence of child poverty in Irish society, pointing out how income inequality shapes the lives of children. Some progress has been made in the last quarter century, with the rate of child poverty, at 15 per cent in 2019, improving by ten percentage points since 1994. However, there has been little improvement between 2008 and 2019.

The National Children's Strategy set targets for outcomes for children. Byrne points out that the national child poverty reduction target set out in 2014, which sought to lift over 70,000 children (aged 0–17) out of consistent poverty by 2020, will not be met, regardless of the impact of the pandemic.

Nevertheless, while a lot less than the target of 70,000, an estimated 14,000 children have been lifted out of consistent poverty between 2011 and 2018. Studies based on analysis of the findings from the *Growing Up in Ireland* study demonstrate time and again that children in families that experience economic stress and/or low income will have poorer outcomes on many measures. Byrne concludes by summarising the challenges that child poverty poses to Irish society and sets out some policy options to address these.

Sinéad Hanafin's contribution discusses the importance of research into the lives of children as an input to policy. She outlines how, in the 1990s, Ireland's data deficit on children and families was such that the United Nations Committee on the Rights of the Child (UNCRC) had expressed significant concern. Hanafin documents the evolution of the National Children's Research Programme 2002–2012, which was set up to address the knowledge gap about children in the context of a 'joined-up' approach to policy that was intended to be child-centred and integrate the many disparate strands of state support.

Hanafin's account of the process of building an evidence base for policy provides a detailed, if sobering, insight into the significant challenges involved. These range from complexities and rigidities in the public system to active resistance, as well as methodological issues related to the availability, quality and harmonisation of data. On the positive side, Hanafin is particularly insightful on the factors that facilitate the process, noting the 'impact of strong support by high-level leaders within the government structure who championed a changed approach and recognised, supported and vigorously promoted the use of evidence in decision-making'. She stresses the importance of the research function being embedded within its government department for the generation and retrieval of evidence for policymaking.

In Chapter 3, Nóirín Hayes examines the evolution of childcare policy and services in Ireland, taking the case of early childhood education and care (ECEC). Her narrative of the extensive activity in this field over the period 1995–2010 chronicles Sylda's far-reaching influence over policy development and investment in ECCE services. Hayes describes the period 2000–2005 as the 'golden age' of the childcare system, where there was extensive policy development, substantial funding and a sense of a clear path toward a sustainable childcare system.

She chronicles the organisational changes of the period, identifying the factors that led to the establishment in 2005 of the Office of the Minister for Children and the strategic thinking that Sylda brought to the process, quoting extensively from an interview with her, published in 2007. While it is acknowledged that no one person can work alone in developing policy, Hayes's paper lucidly demonstrates that it was Sylda's leadership and collaborative style that placed ECEC on the Irish policy map, laying the foundations for the development and growth of the sector. Hayes describes her as a policymaker with vision, drive and energy, whose insights and actions transformed the ECEC landscape in Ireland.

Part II: Putting Policy into Practice – Reaching the Most Vulnerable

As noted above, one of Sylda's strengths was her familiarity with practice and her ability to draw on her experience, both to devise policy and to anticipate the challenges of implementation. In the second part of this volume, we turn our attention to putting policy into practice.

Sylda has always been committed to the profession of social work and the value of the social work perspective in the interface between the state and services for children and families. In Chapter 4, Cormac Quinlan provides a revealing insight into the tightrope walked by social workers who are typically expected to balance rights and navigate the space between private family life and acting on behalf of the state to protect children. The social worker on the ground, guided by the profession's values and ethics and its core foundation in relationship-based practice, seeks to 'do the right thing' in the hope of making a difference to the child and family. There is considerable tension between this and the need to 'do things right' and avoid criticism or failure, by following defined regulated procedures and processes by which performance is frequently measured.

Quinlan suggests key changes that would support building consistent ethical practice and help create a sustainable child protection system. These include legislative and policy reform; promotion of accountability, including a more proactive engagement on understanding good practice and not just reactive responses to perceived failures when they occur; addressing the fragmentation of services and promotion of cross-agency co-operation. The reform of social work practice can be based on wisdom, experience and evidence, but it needs supporting infrastructure to achieve depth and quality. Social workers rely on their practice and their shared values to sustain working relationships and to improve the life of children and families. This requires that the environment and system support good practice, as well as needing social workers to ensure that their approach to practice is consistently embedded with those principles.

In Chapter 5, Ursula Kilkelly reviews the role of public policy in the reform of youth detention in Ireland. She points to the seminal role of the Youth Justice Review of the Children Act, 2001. This Review, commissioned by the Department of Justice, Equality and Law Reform in 2005, and led by Sylda, made a number of far-reaching and pragmatic recommendations, and set out the legal and structural changes required to enhance the delivery of youth justice services in Ireland. Based on consultations with stakeholders and consideration of international trends in youth justice, the Review also emphasised prevention and early intervention. It stressed the need to co-ordinate and integrate services; promote interagency co-operation; and ensure that detention was a last resort, through the resourcing of community-based sanctions.

The youth justice reforms initiated following this Review included reorganisation of youth justice structures to embed them within the national policy framework for children, and the establishment of an Irish Youth Justice Service which was incorporated into the Department of Children and Youth Affairs (DCYA), following the publication of the 'Ryan Report' in 2009, thus strengthening its connection to the wider areas of children's policy. The Ryan Report Implementation Plan (which Sylda oversaw as one of her last tasks prior to her retirement) led to many progressive developments in children's services. It can be said that with protection for children's rights enshrined in the Constitution, a dedicated Minister for Children, a national children's policy framework, and an independent Ombudsman for Children, Ireland is now a leading country in the field of children's rights.

Kilkelly concludes that, while substantial advances have been made in delivering on the national policy priorities in youth justice and detention, limited progress has been made regarding the interface between the state's 'care' and 'justice' systems. There is still some way to go to ensuring that the child-focused approach meets the needs of all troubled children.

Part III: The Citizen and the State – Policy, Governance and Engagement

Perhaps because she was one of the first to enter at a senior level from outside the civil service, Sylda's leadership and operational style was distinctive. Those who worked with her have said that her achievements owe much to a strategic, positive and innovative approach to finding solutions to problems, and an ability to circumvent obstacles to their implementation. She refused to allow traditional/established boundaries to be obstacles and had an ability to inspire and lead her colleagues in the implementation of those solutions.

From her experience of service delivery and community development, and her time in the Office of the Ombudsman, Sylda was acutely conscious of the importance of stakeholder engagement with the policy process, and for service-users to be able to have their voices heard on the issues that affect them. This is evident from the many consultative groups and activities that she initiated, and from her engagement with the community and voluntary sector. In Part III, we take up some of these wider issues of policy delivery and engagement between state and citizen.

In Chapter 6, Dermot McCarthy discusses the search for coherence in policy, looking first at the adoption, more or less explicitly, of paradigms which express the primary objectives of public policy, and which in turn have implications for individual policy domains and the institutions that support them. Against the backdrop of these framing paradigms, he goes on to consider the specific procedures and institutional arrangements that have been developed within the public policy system to promote coherence and consistency in policy formulation and implementation.

McCarthy points out that the creation of a Department for Children (and its successors) has had a significant impact on policy, by developing important new strategies, initiating programmes, and providing sustained high-level political attention to issues relating to children and their wellbeing. Nevertheless, key policies and services that require a cross-departmental approach – such as health, education, income support and housing, as they impact on children – remain outside its remit.

The process of implementation is critical for policy coherence, both in terms of shaping policies as they emerge from central government, and through the cumulative impact of programmes and services on communities and citizens. However, structures of implementation are less than perfect and present a fragmented response to the life experience of those whose needs they address. McCarthy discusses possible strategies for more efficient policy implementation and citizen engagement, and various initiatives that have been more or less successful. He concludes that it is most likely that tensions between policy goals and different organisational requirements will continue to frustrate the ideal of an integrated approach across the relevant areas of public policy and administration. The search for the Holy Grail of joined-up government is unlikely to be successfully concluded, but progress can be made. An abiding focus on coherence is a powerful instrument of policy learning, as is the personal commitment of those in key positions in the system of policy formulation and implementation.

Sylda's experiences of the community and voluntary (C&V) sector ranged from active participation as a founder member of a C&V organisation (Parentline), to working alongside C&V service-providers as a social worker, to engagement with C&V representatives in participatory and voluntary structures at the highest levels of policy-making. In Chapter 7, Mary Murphy analyses the changing policy role of this sector over recent decades, focusing on participation and knowledge as a way of assessing its achievements during the years of social partnership and subsequently.

She reflects on the power dynamics both between the state and the sector, and within the sector itself, drawing particular attention to its gendered nature. She notes that some senior civil servants, many of them women, sought to nurture female leadership and support key actors by advising, nudging, and supporting them along the way. A relatively conscious form of parallel leadership also emerged within the C&V sector, where women supported and enabled each other (even when their respective individual organisations clashed).

Reviewing changes over the past decade, Murphy notes that Irish innovations to facilitate public engagement in the form of Citizens' Assemblies (CAs) have proven effective and broadly acceptable. There are clear examples of the capacity of the C&V sector to influence concrete policy outcomes through these new policy processes, such as the CAs on the Eighth Amendment and on Climate Change. New forms of power and participation are facilitated by contemporary means of instant and horizontal communication so that the future role of civil society in policy development lies in neither consultation nor partnership, but in new modes of participation and knowledge production. These can not only empower actors but also recognise and validate various forms of knowledge for policy.

Eddie Molloy, in Chapter 8, focuses on strengthening the culture of the civil service, which he characterises as the 'fifth estate'. Molloy contends that, when addressing issues of accountability, we need to distinguish structural reform from 'culture' shift, and that this is crucial to understanding the interplay between structure and culture. He cites examples of the existing culture – unwillingness to take personal responsibility, lack of transparency, demonisation of whistle-blowers, or localism in the distribution of public funds – which have a major influence on any formal enquiry, as well as shaping resultant recommendations for improvement. Thus, attempts to design 'best practice' in systems, processes, or legislation are often compromised from the outset. While a great deal of progress in structural reform has been made, the benefits of improvements will not accrue, are offset, or will not be sustained when put under pressure by the existing culture.

Molloy advocates the interrogation and clarification of core values as essential to civil service reform, citing the OECD's 2008 Review of the Irish Public Service and its reference to other countries placing renewed emphasis on rethinking core values, in the context of public management reform.

Sylda became an investigator in the Office of the Ombudsman in 1985, helping to shape the Office in its early days, and to promote its services. In Chapter 9, Emily O'Reilly discusses the role of the Ombudsman in ensuring citizens' rights. She points out that the initial impetus for the establishment of the Irish Office of the Ombudsman was very much about helping the individual person. But the Irish Ombudsman also quickly took on the roles of highlighting systemic problems and of promoting good administration. This means that nowadays when there is a group of complaints which indicate a common underlying problem, the Office will try to ensure that the cause of the problem is addressed. The work of the Office since its establishment, she argues, has led to a transformation in the culture of the public service, from the inward gaze and protection of self, to looking towards the public and their needs.

From the outset, the Ombudsman engaged with systemic problems and injustices in the social welfare system. Examples included the right to equal treatment of men and women in social welfare entitlements (including the right of men to payments as deserted spouses or widowers); interest on delayed social welfare payments; and payment of arrears on late claims for contributory pensions. The Office has been effective in that in almost every case, in the period since 1984, Ombudsman recommendations have been accepted and implemented. O'Reilly also notes periods during which the Ombudsman came under sustained political pressure, which happily came to nought, ensuring that the Office has emerged with both its reputation and independence intact. It has had a high public profile and considerable success both in redressing individual grievances and in contributing substantially to an improved public service.

Epilogue

When Sylda was Director General of the Office for Children and Youth Affairs, she was one of very few women in the top ranks of the civil service. Among that small group, three had been reared in family-owned pubs –

a matter on which Sylda often remarked. Was there something particular about being reared in a pub which shaped them? One of that group, Josephine Feehily, asks whether there were skills that publicans' daughters absorbed that prepared them for a particular way of life. Her observations are witty and wise.

Finally, we are very grateful to the authors who enthusiastically and generously responded to our invitation to contribute to this volume. We believe that the contents provide valuable insights into social policy issues, as well as enlightening readers on some of the hidden and less formal aspects of social policy-making and their impact. We hope that the result provides a fitting tribute to Sylda Langford's contribution to public service in Ireland and that she will enjoy reading the contributions.

PART I

Putting Practice into Policy – Understanding the Needs of Children

CHAPTER 1

INCOME DISTRIBUTION AND INEQUALITY – THE IMPACT ON CHILDREN

Delma Byrne

Introduction

The focus of this chapter is on how income inequality in society shapes the lives of children. Poverty can be defined as a lack of economic resources that prevents a person from participating as an equal in social life. This means that a person can be considered poor if they cannot live a life on par with others in the society in which they live (Sen 1983; Townsend 1979). This chapter begins with a review of trends in the prevalence of child poverty in Irish society, defining children as poor if they live in poor families. There is a strong tradition of analysing trends in the prevalence of child poverty in Irish society (Nolan and Farrell 1990; Callan et al. 2007; Russell, Maître and Nolan 2010) and the second section of this chapter builds on these studies, using the most recently available estimates from the Central Statistics Office. The third section identifies the salience of characteristics of households with children that are associated with poverty risk over time. The fourth section provides an overview of research findings that highlight the impact of poverty and income inequality on children's outcomes. The final section then provides a summary of the challenges that child poverty poses to Irish society, coupled with some policy options.

Trends in the prevalence of child poverty in Irish society

Table 1 shows the most recent estimates of the prevalence of poverty by age-group. For each of the measures shown in Table 1, the child and young adult rates are higher than the rate for working-age adults. Based on relative income poverty, 15 per cent of children aged 0–17 are estimated to be living in poverty in 2019. Furthermore, almost one-in-four children (23 per cent) experience enforced material deprivation, suggesting that these children lack access to items or activities that are typical in society. When poverty measures are combined, 8 per cent of children are exposed to consistent poverty, or poor living standards. When comparing households with and without children, in Table 2, households with children under the age of 18 have higher rates of poverty than households without children.

Table 1: Poverty Measures by Age Group, 2019

	Children	Young Adults	Working-age Adults	Age 65+	Total
60% poverty line	15.3	15.4	11.7	10.5	12.8
Material deprivation	23.3	20.1	16.6	11.2	17.8
Consistent poverty	8.1	6.1	4.9	2.3	5.5

Source: Irish EU-SILC 2019

Table 2: Poverty Measures by Household Type, 2019

	% at Risk of Poverty	% Consistent Poverty
1 adult, with children under 18	29.7	17.1
2 adults with 1–2 children under 18	11.5	5.8
2 adults with 3+ children under 18	13.8	7.9
Other households with children under 18	12.3	4.2
Households without children	11.2	3.5

Source: Irish EU-SILC 2019

This descriptive analysis shows how national poverty rates obscure large variations between adults and children, and families with and without children. We now look to see how each of these poverty indicators has changed over time, using EU-SILC time series data provided by the Central

Statistics Office (CSO). In the analyses below, particular attention is paid to child poverty rates when disaggregated by age-group, and a distinction is made between pre-school children (aged 0–5), primary school children (aged 6–11) and secondary school children (aged 12–17).

Relative income poverty

Figure 1 illustrates the change that has occurred in the poverty risk of people living in Ireland since 2010, the benchmark year against which several national poverty-reduction targets were set. Using the relative income poverty measure, it is clear that poverty risk among the population has improved, particularly after 2015.

Figure 1: Change in the National 'At Risk of Poverty' Rate, Anchored at 2010[1]

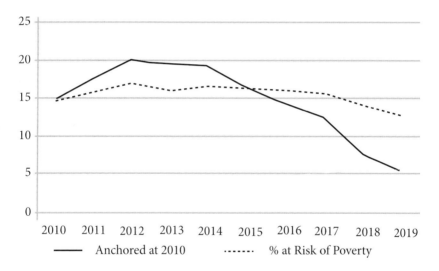

The current rate of child poverty at 15 per cent is considerably lower than the rate in 1994 when one-in-four children experienced poverty (Layte et al. 2006) and in pre-recession 2007 when it was 20 per cent. Figure 2 illustrates little change in the poverty rate of children as a group (age 0–17) between 2008 and 2019. While the share of children living in households experiencing poverty increased between 2008 and 2014, the increase was marginal (a difference of just under two percentage points).

1　The anchored poverty line shows the relative income poverty line that was computed for 2010 and frozen, and allows us to capture changes in poverty.

Figure 2: Children's 'At Risk of Poverty' Rate, by Age Group

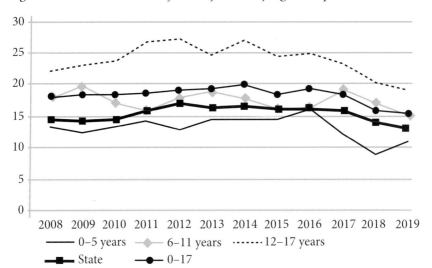

Yet, while aggregate child poverty rates have not varied substantially with changes in the economic cycle, there are significant differences in the experience of child poverty by age-group. That is, poverty risk differs quite substantially by the age group of children, and this is illustrated in Figure 2 over the period 2008–19. A general trend is evident over the period, whereby secondary school-aged children (12–17-year-olds) continue to experience the greatest relative income poverty risk, while both primary and secondary school-aged children experience a poverty risk greater than the population average. In 2017, Ireland had the lowest poverty rate in the EU among children aged 0–5. Pre-school children (aged 0–5) experience the lowest poverty risk, but also show a recent increase in income poverty between 2018 and 2019. Clearly, child poverty in the Irish context is characterised by high rates of poverty among 12–17-year-olds. These older children are also more likely than younger children to live in larger families, migrant families, and households with debt.

Material deprivation

Material deprivation is a subjective measure of material living standards which captures whether families lack access to certain items or activities that are typical in society and whether they are denied access because they cannot afford them. A household is deemed to experience material deprivation – and a certain level of exclusion from society – if it cannot afford two or more of eleven items. As illustrated by Figure 3, children typically experience higher rates of material deprivation than the population average (23 per cent compared to 18 per cent). There are also subtle differences by age as primary and secondary school-aged children (those aged 6–17) experience higher rates than younger children (aged 0–5). Up until 2012, households with primary school-aged children were most likely to indicate an inability to afford items, while after 2012 this became the case for households with secondary school-aged children.

The material conditions of children decreased during the economic recession, reaching a peak in 2013, but had improved between 2014 and 2018. From 2008 to 2013, material deprivation rates rose from 14 per cent to 31 per cent for children aged 0–17. Even when rates of material deprivation fell, children remained most at risk of low living standards. More recently, the material conditions of children have again decreased between 2018 and 2019.

Figure 3: Children's Experience of Material Deprivation, by Age Group

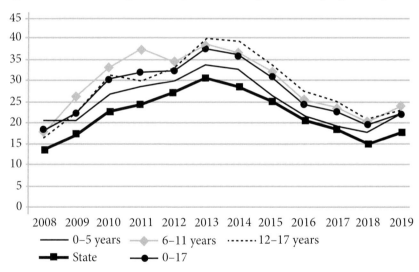

Consistent poverty

A third measure – consistent poverty – is a multidimensional measure of poverty that captures those who are both income poor (with income <60% of median equivalised household disposable income) and those who experience a low standard of living (Callan et al. 1993; Nolan and Whelan 1996). As illustrated by Figure 4, children (aged 0–17) experience higher rates of consistent poverty than the population average. In 2013, rates peaked when 13 per cent of children were at risk of consistent poverty.

Figure 4: Children's Experience of Consistent Poverty, by Age Group

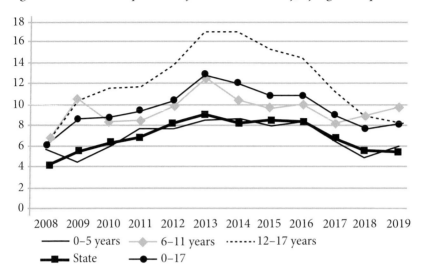

Over time, secondary school-aged children (aged 12–17) typically experience higher rates of consistent poverty than children in other age groups. However, since 2018 and driven by increasing rates of material deprivation, rates among primary school-aged children (aged 6–11) have surpassed those of older children. While consistent poverty was in decline for children and adults between 2013 and 2018, more recently rates of consistent poverty have increased among the 0–5-year-olds (since 2018) and the 6–11-year-olds (since 2017).

A national child poverty reduction target was set out in *Better Outcomes, Brighter Futures: The National Policy Framework for Children and Young People 2014–2020* (DCYA 2014). The target sought to lift over 70,000 children (aged 0–17) out of consistent poverty by 2020, a reduction of at least two-thirds on the 2011 level. However, it has become increasingly clear that efforts have been unsuccessful in reaching this target. Byrne and Treanor (2020) estimate that between 2011 and 2018, 14,000 children have been lifted out of consistent poverty, considerably less than the 70,000 target.[2] Given that rates of consistent poverty among children have increased between 2018 and 2019 and because of the unprecedented employment losses stemming from the pandemic, the child poverty target set for 2020 will not have been

---

2   The share of children (aged 0–17) in consistent poverty decreased from 9.3 per cent in 2011 to 7.7 per cent in 2018, a reduction of 1.6 percentage points (Byrne and Treanor 2020).

reached. Regan and Maître (2020) predict large increases in child income poverty because of the effects of the pandemic. In a scenario where there is an absence of economic recovery, they predict that child income poverty rates will increase between 2.9 and 6 percentage points, while in a scenario of partial economic recovery, the increase in child poverty is more modest (0.2–2.4 percentage points). In either scenario, child poverty rates are predicted to increase.

Poverty Risk: Characteristics of households with children

The descriptive analyses above highlight how a single child poverty rate (aged 0–17) obscures large variations between children based on age group, where older children are at greater risk of poverty than younger children. This section draws from existing research that highlights several key characteristics of households with children that consistently distinguish those who live in poverty from those who do not.

Family structure and age of children

Across all measures of poverty, and controlling for a range of characteristics of households, children living in lone-parent households consistently experience the greatest risk of poverty (Byrne and Treanor 2020; Regan and Maître 2020; Watson et al. 2012; Russell et al. 2010; Layte et al. 2006). Figure 5 shows that while most households with children experienced a decrease in relative income poverty over the period 2010–2019, poverty risk was not experienced equally among all households with children. During this period, the proportion of lone-parent families who were at risk of poverty increased from 25 per cent in 2010 to 40 per cent in 2017. By the end of the period, relative income poverty rates for lone-parent families were five percentage points higher for lone-parent families in 2019 (30 per cent) than in 2010 (25 per cent). Furthermore, a decline from 'peak' poverty risk occurred latest for lone-parent families, after 2017, compared to after 2015 for households with two adults and two children, after 2014 for households with two adults and three children, after 2013 for other households with children and after 2012 for households without children.

Previous research has also found that lone-parent families are considerably more likely to experience a low standard of living compared to two-parent households. By 2013, the material deprivation rate for children in lone-parent households was extremely high, at 64 per cent – twice that of children in two-adult households. By 2018, rates of deprivation had fallen across all household types, but the reduction was lowest for children in lone-parent households (Regan and Maître 2020).

Figure 5: Relative Income Poverty by Household Composition, 2010–2019

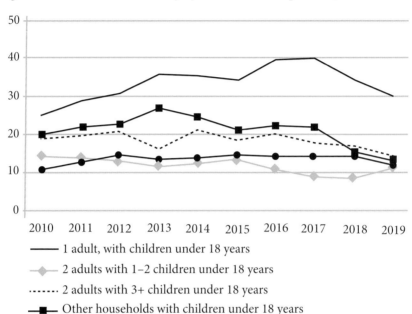

1 adult, with children under 18 years

2 adults with 1–2 children under 18 years

2 adults with 3+ children under 18 years

Other households with children under 18 years

Households without children

Children living in lone-parent families also continue to experience considerably higher rates of consistent poverty than children living in households with two parents, or indeed households without children (Figure 6, opposite). Furthermore, the gap between children living in lone-parent families and those in two-parent families remains high.

In their analyses of the determinants of poverty, Byrne and Treanor (2020) considered the risk of poverty according to the structure of the family in terms of the number and age of children in the family. Their analyses of 2018 EU-SILC data showed that, all else being equal, the age of children in the household matters more than the number of children in the household.[3] That is, households with one or more secondary school-aged children (aged 12–17) are significantly more likely to experience relative income poverty than households with children without secondary school-aged

---

3   It should be noted that the coefficient for families with three or more children approached significance.

children. Households with one or more pre-school children (aged 0–5) are significantly more likely to experience material deprivation than households with children without pre-schoolers. These findings highlight current challenges for government in reducing poverty risk – a disproportionately high poverty risk among children in lone-parent families, and inequalities in poverty risk according to the age of children.

Figure 6: Consistent Poverty by Household Composition, 2008–2019

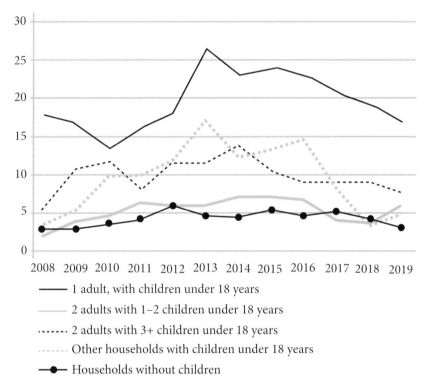

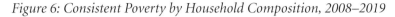

<table>
<tr><td>———</td><td>1 adult, with children under 18 years</td></tr>
<tr><td>———</td><td>2 adults with 1–2 children under 18 years</td></tr>
<tr><td>·······</td><td>2 adults with 3+ children under 18 years</td></tr>
<tr><td>·······</td><td>Other households with children under 18 years</td></tr>
<tr><td>—●—</td><td>Households without children</td></tr>
</table>

Household employment

Previous research consistently identifies that household employment can shape the risk of poverty in terms of either activating poverty or protecting households from poverty risk (Byrne and Treanor 2020; Regan and Maître 2020; Watson et al. 2012; Russell et al. 2010). It is important to note that the relationship between household employment and poverty risk is not entirely straightforward, given that household employment per se does not shield households from poverty risk. This is illustrated by Figure 7, which highlights the relative income poverty rates for all households (with and without children) by the principal economic status of the head of household. Poverty risk among those in employment remains relatively stable across the period, and in 2019, 15 per cent of those in employment experienced poverty, compared to 11 per cent who were unemployed, and 12 per cent of those who were unable to work due to permanent sickness.

Figure 7: Relative Income Poverty Rates by Principal Economic Status, 2008–2019

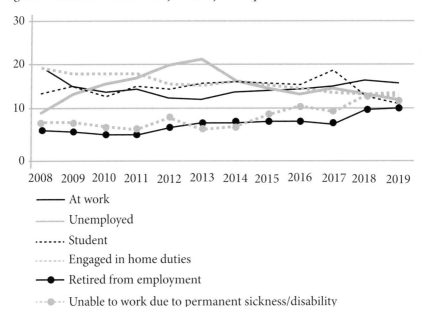

When analyses are restricted to households with children, a general trend is evident whereby relative income poverty and material deprivation rates are consistently highest among unemployed and inactive households (Table 3). As shown by Regan and Maître (2020), the protective role played by parental employment is evident in a reduction in poverty risk between 2008 and 2013 for families where the head of household was in employment. Yet, even when the head of household was employed, there are still large disparities in the experience of poverty between household types, with higher risk of poverty experienced by lone-parent households (Table 4).

Table 3: Risk of Relative Income Poverty and Deprivation by Employment Status in Households with Children

	2008		2013		2018	
	Relative Income Poverty	Deprivation	Relative Income Poverty	Deprivation	Relative Income Poverty	Deprivation
At work	10.6	10.5	8.4	24.7	8.1	12.0
Unemployed	33.8	52.1	46.9	68.7	49.1	49.9
Other/Inactive	40.6	36.2	35.2	56.6	40.4	45.5

Source: Regan and Maître (2020, p. 8)

Table 4: Risk of Relative Income Poverty and Deprivation among Parents in Employment

	2007 & 2008		2013 & 2014		2018	
	Relative Income Poverty	Deprivation	Relative Income Poverty	Deprivation	Relative Income Poverty	Deprivation
1 adult with children	19.9	27.5	15.1	52.1	18.6	29.5
2 adults with 1–3 children	8.4	8.3	5.8	20.6	4.9	9.6
Other households with children	14.3	8.9	15.5	27.6	14.1	16.5

Source: Regan and Maître (2020, p. 21)

Another way of conceptualising the economic situation of households relates to the work intensity of the household, which considers the labour force status of all adults in the household. Using a measure developed by Eurostat,[4] research finds that children living in jobless or low-work-intensity households are significantly more likely to experience relative income poverty, material deprivation and consistent poverty, all else being equal (Byrne and Treanor 2020; Regan and Maître 2020). As shown by Table 5, households with children that have very low work intensity are increasingly exposed to poverty risk over time. Ireland compares unfavourably with other European countries given the comparatively high share of children living in households with very low work intensity.

---

4   The level of work intensity of the household captures the amount of available worktime spent at work by potential earners in a household (European Commission 2010).

Table 5: Risk of Relative Income Poverty and Deprivation by Work Intensity

	2007 & 2008		2013 & 2014		2018	
	Relative Income Poverty	Deprivation	Relative Income Poverty	Deprivation	Relative Income Poverty	Deprivation
Very low work intensity	56.6	52.2	57.7	74.5	62.7	61.0
Low	28.5	35.7	26.0	58.7	34.7	**
Medium	15.7	15.6	12.5	32.6	15.0	21.0
High/Very high	5.8	7.3	3.7	19.1	4.7	8.5

** *Numbers too small to report*
Source: *Regan and Maître (2020, p. 8)*

Parental characteristics and emerging trends

The section above highlights some of the longer-term social processes that underlie poverty risk. Several other well-known socio-demographics that are associated with poverty risk are discussed here: parental education and parental health. Higher levels of education have long been viewed as a buffer against poverty – research consistently finds that low levels of education are predictive of poverty risk (Russell et al. 2010). In 2018, 16 per cent of children living in a household headed by an adult with a low education level (lower secondary or less) were at risk of relative income poverty, 23 per cent were at risk of material deprivation and 14 per cent experienced consistent poverty. The incidence of chronic health and activity-limiting conditions among parents is also, over time, a well-established determinant of poverty risk in households with children (Russell et al. 2010; Byrne and Treanor 2020). In regression models that include a measure of the work intensity of households with children, the effect of low work intensity absorbs the influence of poor health and low education on the risk of consistent poverty (Byrne and Treanor 2020), given that these groups are most likely to live in low-work-intensity households.

Previous research highlighted that in the mid-1990s, there were significant differences in the poverty risk (both relative income poverty and material deprivation) of households with children, depending on whether the head of household held Irish nationality or nationality from another country (Russell et al. 2010). More recently, analyses of 2018 data show that all else being equal, households with children that are headed by a migrant experience a greater risk of relative income poverty than households with children in all other households (Byrne and Treanor 2020). In the Irish context, much less attention has been paid to how child poverty operates along migration, minority ethnic, or racial lines than in other country contexts.

Child poverty and children's outcomes

There is a vast body of research internationally that highlights how child poverty is associated with lower child wellbeing, and long-term negative effects (Bellani and Bia 2019; Yang 2019; Lesner 2018). Given an increasing availability of longitudinal data, including the *Growing Up in Ireland* study, we are now moving towards a better understanding of how poverty impacts multiple domains of children's lives in Ireland. In the section below, a selection of Irish research findings on the association between child poverty and children's outcomes is discussed. Duncan and Le Menestrel (2019) offer a useful way to conceptualise how poverty may influence children's development and outcomes, by identifying two key mechanisms that can be applied to the Irish context:

- The first relates to 'what money can buy' – how poverty shapes parent/guardian access to goods and services that are known to enhance child development and outcomes.
- The second relates to the negative effect that poverty has on exposure to environmental stressors that a family may experience, which in turn influences child development and outcomes.

Meeting children's basic needs: Food and shelter

In the research literature, access to services and communal resources is viewed as essential to improving the lives of children living in poverty. Research has found that poverty impacts access to essential goods such as food and housing, as families living in poverty are more likely to face food poverty (Healy 2019) and are likely to experience lower housing quality (Corrigan and Watson 2018) and threats to housing stability (Hearn 2011). High housing costs are associated with poorer cognitive outcomes for children in other country contexts (Newman and Holupka 2014). Child poverty rates are particularly pronounced in households with children where the home is rented as opposed to in households where the home is owner-occupied (Byrne and Treanor 2020).

Access to services during childhood: Education and health

Research in the Irish context highlights the social stratification of access to nonparental childcare, and how high-income families are more likely to use multiple forms of childcare (Byrne and O'Toole 2015). In contrast, low-income families that spend a greater proportion of their disposable income on childcare compared to high-income families (Russell et al. 2018) are more likely to send their child to school at an earlier age, and are more likely to indicate that they would have been unable to send their child to preschool in the absence of the early childhood care and education scheme (ECCE) (McGinnity, Russell and Murray 2015). This body of research finds that universal access to early childhood care and education enables all parents to meet these early education and care needs, but that childcare costs are a strong barrier to hours spent in paid work, particularly among low-income families (Russell et al. 2018). The authors also conclude that exclusion from the labour market due to childcare costs is likely to influence poverty risk and household joblessness.

Layte and Nolan (2015) report that eligibility for free GP care affects children's use of GP services, showing how healthcare entitlement structures impact on children's use of health services. Furthermore, the relationship between income poverty and health poverty is well established in the Irish context (Madden 2011; Layte, Nolan and Nolan 2006) and research shows that children of mothers with low levels of education are at greatest risk of childhood obesity (Madden 2017). Burke (2020) highlights an association between the psychological health of children and parental ability to make ends meet. Nolan and Smyth (2020) report that health behaviours of 17-year-olds are stratified by family social class background, family structure and parental education levels.[5]

Developmental and educational outcomes

Research in other country contexts finds that having more money directly improves the development and level of achievement of children (Cooper and Stewart 2013). While few studies in the Irish context examine the relationship between the poverty measures highlighted in the earlier section of this chapter and children's developmental and educational outcomes, low income and economic stress appear to demonstrate a causal effect, particularly on cognitive and developmental outcomes. In line

---

5   They identified three groups of 17-year-olds based on their health behaviours – the 'unhealthy smokers and drinkers', the 'unhealthy diet and physical activity' group and a 'healthy' group.

with international studies, research drawing on GUI data finds that low household income is associated with children's development from infancy to middle childhood.[6] Children living in families that experience economic stress and/or low income are significantly more likely to demonstrate poorer cognitive and developmental outcomes at age three and at age five (Byrne and O'Toole 2015; McGinnity et al. 2015; McGinnity et al. 2017). All else being equal, low income has less of an effect on children's socio-emotional outcomes by age five (Russell, Kenny and McGinnity 2016).

Access to early childhood care and education has implications for reducing inequalities in children's outcomes, but the effect on children's developmental outcomes is small and varies by childcare type. Byrne and O'Toole (2015) report that childcare type during infancy (at nine months) is associated with some developmental outcomes by age three. While there is an effect of childcare type at age three on children's cognitive and socio-emotional development by age five, the effects are reported to be small (Russell, Kenny and McGinnity 2016; McGinnity et al. 2017).[7]

Among older children, McCoy et al. (2016) used the GUI data to examine the role of family economic vulnerability on child self-concept and academic skill development. While they find no influence of family economic vulnerability on child self-concept, children who were living in households that were deemed to be economically vulnerable in wave 1 (at age 9) were more likely to be in the lowest numeric ability quintile by age 13, all else being equal.

The quality of children's lives: Access to enrichment activities

Low income also extends to influence the quality of children's lives and activities. Previous research has found that household income is a barrier to children participating in structured cultural activities (at age 9 and at age 13), given that many cultural activities outside of school require payment. Children who engage in these paid activities outside of the home and school also experience higher scores in maths and reading, and higher scores on a range of child wellbeing outcomes (Smyth 2016; McCoy, Byrne, and Banks 2011). Higher income in families facilitates more investment in enrichment and cognitively stimulating activities such as constructive use of books and computers in the home.

---

6   This is also the case for low levels of household employment, low parental education, family stress and poor maternal health.

7   This research finds that children who are cared for by relatives at age three have lower socio-emotional outcomes at age five, and that children who are cared for by non-relatives have fewer socio-emotional difficulties than children in other care settings (Russell, Kenny and McGinnity 2016).

Family stress and child development

The second approach, the stress mechanism, draws on research that highlights how economic hardship can increase psychological distress in families, including children, and decrease emotional wellbeing for both parents/guardians and children. It is argued that psychological stress may manifest in parenting behaviour, family stress or marital conflict, which in turn influence or shape children's cognitive and socio-emotional outcomes and general wellbeing (Conger and Elder 1994; Conger and Conger 2002). In the Irish context, research has identified a direct association between low household income and maternal stress scores, low household income and emotional behavioural adjustment, and low household income and mother–child conflict (Nixon 2012; Nixon, Swords and Murray 2013). Watson et al. (2014; 2015) also report a strong association between economic vulnerability and negative socio-emotional outcomes among children. Persistent economic vulnerability was most detrimental to children in terms of their socio-emotional development (Watson et al. 2015).

The family stress model argues that there is an indirect association between the resources in the home and children's cognitive or psychological development via parental experience of economic strain and psychological distress. Layte (2017) reports that the family stress model can explain variations in children's cognitive ability at age 7 but is limited as an explanation for variations in children's psychological adjustment (Layte and McCrory 2018).

Challenges and policy options

Previous Irish research has found that rates of poverty among children increased sharply during the 1970s and 1980s and remained high by the mid-1990s when one-in-four children experienced poverty (Layte et al. 2006). Since then, rates of relative income poverty among children have been in decline, reducing to 20 per cent by 2007, rising a little during the recessionary years, but showing a general pattern of decline after 2014. While rates of child poverty in Ireland remain lower than the European average, 15 per cent of children (aged 0–17) living in Ireland – three-in-twenty – do not live life on a par with their peers. More recently, rates of material deprivation or low living standards among children show an increase between 2018 and 2019. These patterns come at a time when government attempts to reduce child poverty to targets set in 2014 have been unsuccessful, and the pandemic brings with it predictions of an increase in child poverty rates in the coming years.

The descriptive data presented in graphs and tables in this chapter highlight several current challenges in reducing child poverty. Clearly, an aggregate child poverty rate obscures large variation in poverty risk between children, particularly in terms of relative income poverty and consistent poverty. Over time, secondary school-aged children continue to experience the greatest risk of income poverty, material deprivation and consistent poverty, as families with one or more secondary school-aged children are more likely to experience poverty. At the same time, pre-school children experience the lowest poverty risk in Europe. These findings suggest that policy measures that were taken to reduce child poverty among very young children were successful. However, this same commitment needs to be extended to all groups of children, particularly older children. It is evident that policy actions to reduce child poverty should adopt a life-course approach in seeking to reduce age-related child poverty. In other institutional contexts, such as the Nordic countries, there is much less variation in poverty risk across age groups of children. In line with recommendations from the National Economic and Social Council (2020), priority should be given to improving child income support, but with consideration of the age of children in the family.

The data also highlight how national poverty rates obscure variation between families with and without children, as families with children face the greatest risk of poverty. However, over time, this risk of poverty among families with children is consistently disproportionately experienced by children living in lone-parent families. This is also the case for children living in households with very low work intensity, children living in households with low parental education levels, poor parental health and where the head of household has migrated to Ireland. The salience of these trends over time suggests that the current social welfare system is finding it difficult to meet changing patterns of household and family formation and to support labour market participation of parents with caring responsibilities (NESC 2020).[8] An emergent pattern from the data reveals how children living in families headed by a parent with a recent migrant history experience a greater risk of poverty, all else being equal. Given that children and young adults make

---

8   Income maximisation is a strategy that is used in Scotland to maximise the incomes of people living in poverty, and is a requirement under the Child Poverty (Scotland) Act, 2017. It is a service that looks at people's entitlements and advises them with a co-ordinated response across sectors (Treanor 2020).

up most members of minority ethnic populations in Ireland (Byrne and Treanor 2020), this issue needs to be urgently addressed by both policy and research.

A reduction in poverty demands investment in public spending beyond welfare spending and supporting labour market participation, as low-income families require access to education, health and a range of supports to help lift them out of poverty. OECD (2018) emphasises that a range of approaches is required to reduce child poverty. These include:

- Welfare strategies that seek to target benefits and cash transfers at low-income families. The OECD advocates an increase in social spending to ensure that social benefits grow at the same rate as wages to reduce the poverty rate of jobless families and single-parent families. OECD also advocates an increase in social transfers for working and non-working households, while maintaining average work incentives at the bottom of the income distribution (Cantillon et al. 2017);
- Work strategies and policies that seek to improve access and remove the barriers to employment and incentivise employment, more individualised support to assist hard-to-place workers and help parents in low-income families to improve their education and skill levels and access better-quality jobs. OECD recommends that work strategies should make work pay and ensure that the tax/benefit system provides incentives to work;
- Family-spending strategies that seek to target a mix of cash transfer and in-kind benefits, particularly for low-income families, towards households, to enhance access to affordable high-quality all-day childcare. OECD data show that public investment in family spending in Ireland was still in decline in 2016, well after the 2008–13 recessionary years had passed.

Several policy mechanisms that span a range of government departments are required to produce a reduction in child poverty. A multidimensional approach to the reduction of child poverty will require continuing emphasis on a cross-departmental approach among departments that support public policies for families and children. A more active focus on child-poverty reduction than has been previously considered could be achieved through devising a comprehensive anti-poverty strategy that captures the wider range of policies that seek to improve the lives of families with children living in poverty.

References

Bellani, L., and Bia, M. (2019), 'The Long-run Effect of Childhood Poverty and the Mediating Role of Education', *Journal of the Royal Statistical Society*, vol. 181, no. 1, pp 37–68.

Burke, L.A. (2020), 'Child Psychological Health During the Great Recession in Ireland', *The Economic and Social* Review, vol. 51, no. 4, pp 489–506.

Byrne, D., and O'Toole, C. (2015), *The Influence of Childcare Arrangements on Child Well Being from Infancy to Middle Childhood*, Dublin: TUSLA in association with Maynooth University.

Byrne, D., and Treanor, M. (2020), *Income, Poverty and Deprivation among Children: A Statistical Baseline Analysis*, Dublin: Department of Children and Youth Affairs.

Callan, T., Coleman, K., Nolan, B., and Walsh, J.R. (2007), *Child Poverty and Child Income Supports: Ireland in Comparative Perspective*, Dublin: The Economic and Social Research Institute.

Cantillon, B., Chzhen, Y., Handa, S., and Nolan, B. (2017), *Children of Austerity: Impact of the Great Recession on Child Poverty in Rich Countries*, Oxford: Oxford University Press.

Conger, R.D., and Conger, K.J. (2002), 'Resilience in Midwestern Families: Selected Findings from the First Decade of a Prospective, Longitudinal Study', *Journal of Marriage and the Family*, vol. 64, pp 361–73.

Conger, R.D., and Elder, G.H.J. (1994), *Families in Troubled Times: Adapting to Change in Rural America*, Hawthorne, NY: De Gruyter Aldine.

Cooper, K., and Stewart, K. (2013), *Does Money Affect Children's Outcomes? A Systematic Review*, York: Joseph Rowntree Foundation.

Corrigan, E., and Watson, D. (2018), 'Social Housing in the Irish Housing Market', ESRI Working Paper No. 594, June.

Department of Children and Youth Affairs (DCYA) (2014), *Better Outcomes, Brighter Futures: The National Policy Framework for Children and Young People 2014–2020*, Dublin: Department of Children and Youth Affairs.

Duncan, G., and Le Menestrel, S. (2019), *A Roadmap to Reducing Child Poverty*, Washington, DC: The National Academies Press.

European Commission (2010), *The European Platform Against Poverty and Social Exclusion: A European Framework for Social and Territorial Cohesion*, Brussels: European Commission.

Feazer, H., and Marlier, E. (2007), *Tackling Child Poverty and Promoting the Social Inclusion of Children in the EU: Key Lessons Synthesis Report,*

European Commission DG Employment, Social Affairs and Equal Opportunities.

Healy, A.E. (2019), 'Measuring Food Poverty in Ireland: The Importance of Including Exclusion', *Irish Journal of Sociology*, vol. 27, no. 2, pp 105–27.

Hearn, R. (2011), *Public Private Partnerships in Ireland: Failed Experiment or the Way Forward for the State*, Manchester: Manchester University Press.

Layte, R. (2017), 'Why Do Working-Class Kids Do Worse in School? An Empirical Test of Two Theories of Educational Disadvantage', *European Sociological Review*, vol. 33, no. 4, pp 489–503.

Layte, R., and McCrory, C. (2018), 'Fiscal Crises and Personal Troubles: The Great Recession in Ireland and Family Processes', *Social Psychiatry and Psychiatric Epidemiology*, vol. 53, pp 987–1001.

Layte, R., and Nolan, A. (2015), 'Eligibility for Free GP Care and the Utilisation of GP Services by Children in Ireland', *International Journal of Health Economics and Management*, vol. 15, pp 3–27.

Layte, R., Maître, B., Nolan, B., and Whelan, C.T. (2006), *Day in Day Out: Understanding the Dynamics of Child Poverty*, Dublin: Institute of Public Administration/Combat Poverty Agency.

Layte, R., Nolan, A., and Nolan, B. (2007), *Poverty and Access to Community Health Services*, Dublin: Combat Poverty Agency.

Lesner, R.V. (2018), 'The Long-Term Effect of Childhood Poverty', *Journal of Population Economics*, vol. 31, no. 3, pp 969–1004.

McCoy, S., Byrne, D., and Banks, J. (2011), 'Too Much of a Good Thing? Gender 'Concerted Cultivation' and Unequal Achievement in Primary Education', *Child Indicators Research*, vol. 5, pp 155–78.

McCoy, S., Maitre, B., Watson, D. and, Banks, J. (2016), 'The Role of Parental Expectations in Understanding Social and Academic Well-being Among Children with Disabilities in Ireland', *European Journal of Special Needs Education*, vol. 31, pp 535–52.

McGinnity, F., Russell, H., and Murray, A. (2015), *Non-Parental Childcare and Child Cognitive Outcomes at Age 5*, Dublin: The Economic and Social Research Institute.

McGinnity, F., McMullin, P., Murray, A., and Russell, H. (2017), 'Social Inequality in Cognitive Outcomes in Ireland: What is the Role of the Home Learning Environment and Childcare?' in Blossfeld, H.P., Kulic, N., Skopek, J., and Triventi, M. (eds), *Childcare, Early Education and Social Inequality: An International Perspective*, Cheltenham, UK, Northampton, MA: Edward Elgar, pp 109–32.

Madden, D. (2011), 'Health and Income Poverty in Ireland, 2003–2006', *The Journal of Economic Inequality*, vol. 9, no. 1, pp 23–33.

Madden, D. (2017), 'Childhood Obesity and Maternal Education in Ireland', *Economics and Human Biology,* vol. 27, pp 114–25.

NESC (2020), *The Future of the Irish Social Welfare System: Participation and Protection*, Dublin: National Economic and Social Development Office.

Newman, S.J., and Holupka, C.S. (2014), 'Housing Affordability and Investments in Children', *Journal of Housing Economics*, vol. 24, pp 89–100.

Nixon, E. (2012), *How Families Matter for Social and Emotional Outcomes of 9-Year-Old Children*, Dublin: Department of Children and Youth Affairs.

Nixon, E., Swords L., and Murray, A. (2013), *Parenting and Infant Development, Infant Cohort. Report 3*, Dublin: The Stationery Office/ Department of Children and Youth Affairs.

Nolan, A., and Smyth, E. (2020), *Clusters of Health Behaviours Among Young Adults in Ireland*, Dublin: ESRI Research Series 101.

Nolan, B., and Farrell, B. (1990), *Child Poverty in Ireland*, Dublin: Combat Poverty Agency.

Nolan, B., and Whelan, C.T. (1996), *Resources, Deprivation and Poverty*, Oxford: Oxford University Press.

Regan, M., and Maître, B. (2020), *Child Poverty in Ireland and the Pandemic Recession*, Budget Perspectives, No 2021/4, Dublin: The Economic and Social Research Institute.

Russell, H., Maître, B., and Nolan, B. (2010), *Monitoring Poverty Trends in Ireland 2004–2007: Key Issues for Children, People of Working Age and Older People*, ESRI Research Series, no. 17, August, Dublin: The Economic and Social Research Institute.

Russell, H., Kenny, O., and McGinnity, F. (2016), *Childcare, Early Education and Socio-Emotional Outcomes at Age 5: Evidence from the Growing Up in Ireland Study*, Dublin: The Economic and Social Research Institute in association with Pobal.

Russell, H., McGinnity, F., Fahey, E., and Kenny, O. (2018), *Maternal Employment and the Costs of Childcare in Ireland*, Dublin: The Economic and Social Research Institute in association with Pobal.

Sen, A. (1983), 'Poor, Relatively Speaking', *Oxford Economic Papers*, vol. 35, no. 2, pp 153–69.

Smyth, E. (2016), *Arts and Cultural Participation Among Children and Young People: Insights from the Growing up in Ireland Study*, Dublin: The Arts Council.

Townsend, P. (1979), *Poverty in the United Kingdom*, Harmondsworth: Penguin.

Treanor, M. (2020), *Child Poverty: Aspiring to Survive*, Bristol: Policy Press.

Watson, D., Maître, B., and Whelan, C.T. (2012), *Understanding Childhood Deprivation in Ireland*, Dublin: The Economic and Social Research Institute.

Watson, D., Maître, B., Whelan, C.T., and Williams, J. (2014), *Dynamics of Child Economic Vulnerability and Socio-Emotional Development: An Analysis of the First Two Waves of the Growing up in Ireland Study*, Dublin: Department of Children and Youth Affairs.

Watson, D., Whelan, C.T., Maître, B., and Williams, J. (2015), 'Family Economic Vulnerability and the Great Recession: An Analysis of the First Two Waves of the Growing up in Ireland Study', *Longitudinal and Life Course Studies*, vol. 6, no. 3, pp 230–44.

Yang, Z. (2019), 'Measurement of Childhood Poverty in the United States and its Enduring Influences', *Journal of Sociology & Social Welfare*, vol. 46, no. 2, pp 47–73.

CHAPTER 2

Reflections on Building an Evidence Base Around Children's Lives

Sinéad Hanafin

The importance of evidence for public policy

In this post-truth world, where 'alternative facts' and the spread of disinformation are endemic in our society, it has never been more important to ensure that scientifically generated knowledge is readily available to decision-makers (Higgins 2016; Hasen 2019). This is particularly true for government organisations, and Shaxson (2005) identifies a number of reasons why evidence in policy-making is necessary. These include being able a) to understand the policy environment and how it is it is impacted by various policy options; b) to identify linkages between strategic direction and implementation in practice; c) to recognise what is required to meet strategic goals; and d) to influence stakeholders to assist in achieving policy imperatives.

The term 'evidence' itself is contested, however, and what counts as evidence is often dependent not only on the methodological position regarding the hierarchy of evidence (systematic reviews and meta-analyses, randomised controlled trials, cohort studies, case-control studies, cross-sectional surveys, case reports), but also on stakeholder viewpoint. Academics focus on scientific evidence generated through systematic methodologies, while others draw from a much broader landscape. A range of sources has been identified as informing decisions by policy-makers and service-providers, and these include local data, practice guidelines, personal contacts, personal experience and expertise, pragmatics and lobbyists (Shaxson 2005; Oliver and de Vocht 2017). Irrespective of stakeholder, methodological, ontological or epistemological position, it is clear that an absence of evidence can lead to significant challenges in decision-making. These challenges have been acknowledged in the Irish context for some time now and there is some agreement that access to robust information is essential to good decision-making (National Statistics Board 2015; Health Research Board 2016; Science Foundation Ireland 2012), as well as to economic growth and development (National Competitiveness Council 2015; Enterprise Ireland 2012). A commitment to using evidence to inform policy-making is clearly reflected in strategic developments across different sectors (Enterprise Ireland 2012; Lee, Cyganiak and Decker 2014) and populations (Department of Health 2013; Department of Children and Youth Affairs 2011).

This chapter focuses on one such strategic development, which took place in the context of the implementation of the National Children's Strategy (NCS) (Government of Ireland 2000), which had three goals. Goal 1 focused on giving children a voice in matters that affected them, Goal 2 on understanding children's lives better, and Goal 3 on ensuring that children would receive high-quality supports and services. Goal 2, understanding children's lives, took place against the backdrop of a 'significant concern' identified in the concluding comments of the 1998 United Nations Committee on the Rights of the Child (UNCRC) report (UNCRC 1998), where the committee highlighted:

> certain lacunae in the statistical and other information collected by the State party, including with respect to the selection and development of indicators to monitor the implementation of the principles and provisions of the Convention. (p. 4)

This concern was followed by a recommendation for Ireland to develop a data system around children's lives, which was inclusive of all children and which had a specific emphasis on vulnerable children. The committee also highlighted a need for disaggregated data to be gathered and analysed, in order to assess programme implementation. In addition to statistical lacunae, Langford (2007) noted that historically there had been relatively little research on children and childhood in Ireland, and in terms of policy development there had been a reliance on research based in other jurisdictions.

Arising from these knowledge deficits, a National Children's Research Programme 2002–2012 was designed and implemented. The objectives of the programme were:

- To build a more coherent understanding of children's development and needs among those working with children
- To develop an evidence-based approach to decision-making at all levels down to the point of service delivery
- To improve the commissioning, production and dissemination of research and information, and
- To improve evaluation and monitoring of children's services.

Breaking out of the silo

Konrad Zacharias, a Nobel prizewinner, is credited with saying that 'experts are people who know more and more about less and less, until they know everything about nothing'. While it is doubtful that this is an accurate reflection of the sum of what experts know, it is undoubtedly true to say that the more expert a person becomes, the greater their focus is on one particular issue or area to the exclusion of other areas. This is replicated in how policy-makers and practitioners reflect their particular areas of responsibility. Those working in health privilege knowledge about health services, epidemiology, morbidity and mortality, while those in education do so in respect of education services, children's cognitive outcomes and educational progress. To generate a sustainable evidence base around children's lives that has relevance to all aspects of all children's lives, however, requires a more holistic approach. In Ireland, this holistic approach was set out in the NCS (Government of Ireland 2000), the development of which took place in response to considerable criticisms about a fragmented approach to children's policies and services and a failure of national and local organisations to work together in the best interests of the child (UNCRC 1998).

Integrated and joined-up understandings of children's lives

The development of the NCS marked the inauguration of a period of extensive and unprecedented policy development around children's lives that has continued up to this day. As a way of adopting a more integrated approach, the strategy, its goals and actions were underpinned and informed by a conceptualisation of children referred to as the Whole Child Perspective. This perspective drew on Bronfenbrenner's bio-ecological model (Bronfenbrenner 1979; Bronfenbrenner and Morris 1998) and also underpinned the national children's research programme.

At the core of this perspective is an explication of the socio-ecological environment within which children live; an acknowledgement of the multi-dimensionality of their lives; a focus on the formal and informal supports available to them; and a recognition of the importance of relationships around them. Central to these understandings is a clear recognition that children are active participants in their own lives, with a right to a voice, and that their development and outcomes are a complex interaction between their own interlinked capacities, the environment within which they live and the interventions that take place in their lives. This understanding, along with more recent developments in respect of life-course theory, continues to inform national policies and practices in Ireland around children today (Murphy et al. 2019).

This conceptualisation of children and young people's lives is also reflected in the cross-cutting policy structures put in place following publication of the NCS. This structure has grown over the last twenty years, from the National Children's Office (NCO), to the Office of the Minister for Children (OMC), Office of the Minister for Children and Youth Affairs (OMCYA), Department of Children and Youth Affairs (DCYA), and finally in 2020 the Department of Children, Equality, Disability, Integration and Youth (DCEDIY). Kaoukji and Little (2007, p. 67), in an interview with Sylda Langford, Director General of the OMCYA, noted that structural developments that emerged from the NCS were 'the first joined-up piece of Government executive' to take place in Ireland, and this in turn led to a requirement for an evidence base about all children that was both holistic and comprehensive.

Implementation of a national research programme

The implementation of the programme took place though four discrete but interrelated components which operated in a complementary manner to achieve the objectives outlined above. These four components were:

1   A strategic approach to the development of the data and statistical
      infrastructure around children's lives, which included three

components viz the development of a national set of child wellbeing indicators (Hanafin et al. 2007), the biennial publication of the *State of the Nation's Children Report* (OMC 2006; OMCYA 2008, 2010) and the development of a National Strategy for Research and Data on Children's Lives (Department of Children and Youth Affairs, 2011);

2   A funded research programme where targeted studies across different areas of children's lives were commissioned from researchers based in a variety of different institutions. Twenty-eight studies, including the National Longitudinal Study of Children *(Growing up in Ireland)* which followed the progress of about 20,000 children, were commissioned under this strand of the programme;

3   A capacity-building programme which provided funding for Masters by research, PhDs and research placements within the policy structure, seed funding for academic programmes such as the PhD in Child and Youth Research led by the Children's Research Centre at Trinity College Dublin and the Child and Family Research Centre, and core funding for the Children's Research Centre at Trinity College Dublin;

4   A knowledge transfer programme which included research launches with strong media presence, seminars to showcase the work of PhD and Masters scholars, as well as a set of briefing notes on funded research projects and completed theses. In addition, a database of research including material on child protection and welfare, children in detention, interagency working, and child health was created. Throughout the period of this programme, direct research support was provided to policy-makers within the OMCYA, developing national policy on play, recreation, early-years care and education and child protection, as well as providing briefing material and responses to parliamentary questions, and research input to departmental responses on a wide range of policy issues relevant to children's lives.

Challenges when building an evidence base

Different perspectives

The implementation of these developments was challenging and, at times, frustratingly slow, complex and problematic due to the cross-cutting nature of the work, and also due to the specialist nature of research within a generalist civil service. Interdepartmental challenges arose, particularly in commissioning research or reporting on data where another department or organisation had overall responsibility for that specific area. Lessons learnt early in the implementation of the programme resulted in a collaborative approach to commissioning research and identifying data. Despite this, changes in personnel across other organisations or government departments, or findings from research where the results reflected negatively on the relevant policy-making department could, and did, result in delays in publication. One report that had already been printed, for example, could not be launched until the following year. Another report lay on the desk of a senior policy-maker for over a year due to the timing of policy discussions underway internationally about the subject area.

Gaps in knowledge about what was already available

Another issue arose in respect of a lack of knowledge about data and research already available. This was across multiple stakeholders and was evident in submissions made during the consultation process for the *National Strategy for Research and Data on Children's Lives*. In some of these cases, the positioning of the research team within a government department meant an awareness of actions already in place to meet a particular need or actions planned for the future which were not widely known about. In other cases, however, data that were publicly and readily available were deemed too difficult to collect. One example related to alcohol and drug use by young people where data had been collected from children since the mid–1980s through two international studies — European School Survey Project on Alcohol and Other Drugs (ESPAD 2020) and Health Behaviour in School-Aged Children (Hibell et al. 2000). During the course of a consultation workshop in 2010 around the development of the *National Strategy for Research and Data on Children's Lives*, it was declared that not only were these data unavailable, but that even seeking to collect such data from children under eighteen years would not be possible because of legal issues due to children's ages. Discussions taking place at that workshop were also severely hampered because of an unwillingness of the national policy-making department to allow another organisation to make recommendations to fill data and research gaps in that particular sector. In summary, differences between the two communities of researchers and policy-makers in terms of purpose, viewpoints and understanding of evidence were never far from the reality of implementing a national programme of research and data from within government.

The State of the Nation's Children Report: *Methodological challenges*

A number of methodological challenges also arise. These were technically complex and were especially problematic in the case of the compilation of the *State of the Nation's Children Report* where data were drawn from twenty-two different data sources relating to multiple areas of children's lives (Hanafin and Brooks 2009). Issues related to the availability, quality, harmonisation and disaggregation of data, including time trend data. Examples of issues arising include:

- *Availability of data*, which included: an absence of any data in respect of some areas of children's lives (e.g. children's nutritional outcomes including BMI); an unequal distribution in the availability of data across different age groups (it was particularly lacking in the middle childhood period) and indicator areas (especially in respect of subjective wellbeing); lack of comprehensiveness when reporting on the indicator area (e.g. information on public expenditure on children was available only for that relating to education); and lack of availability of some data over different time periods (e.g. three indicators based on data from the Programme for International Student Assessment study had not been included in the 2003 data collection, meaning that the 2006 *State of the Nation's Children* reported on data from 2000 for these indicators).
- *Quality of the data available,* particularly in respect of the extent to which the data source provided national coverage (e.g. the National Intellectual Disability Database at that time related to only about 70 per cent coverage of the population); and the timeliness of the data (e.g. a number of demographic variables in the 2006 *State of the Nation's Children Report* were based on the 2002 Census); comparability of the information between different geographical areas (e.g. administrative data relating to screening for growth and development by Public Health Nurses was based on different meta-data across different HSE areas); and the level of certainty regarding the accuracy of the information. While survey data are generally collected using a well-developed questionnaire that has been pre-tested and validated for use with a specific population, this is not the case in respect of administrative data which often operate to support day-to-day service implementation. Understandably, the reliability and validity of administrative data are

likely to be considerably lower, but the extent to which there are other problems in the data is often not known.

- *Harmonisation of variables,* especially in respect of demographic considerations such as social class and geographic classifications and the application of international or national measures. At that time, issues such as an absence of a postcode to support spatial analysis and the absence of a unique patient identifier with electronic records for health services were identified as critical, but absent, parts of a statistical infrastructure. While a postcode is now in place, little progress has been made in respect of a unique patient identifier or electronic health records, despite extensive considerations. The Personal Public Service Number (PPS) issued by the Client Identity Services (CIS) at the Department of Social Protection is now in use across a number of public service agencies and this holds out opportunities for data linkages over time, provided GDPR challenges can be overcome.

- *Disaggregation of data,* which varied depending on the data source. For some data sources, data were accessible in respect of age, gender, social class and geography, while for others, particularly those drawn from administrative data sources or studies focusing on one age group only (e.g. Programme for International Student Assessment which includes only 15-year-olds). As noted above, some data were available only for a particular time period (e.g. screening for health and development at that time referred to one time period only — 48 hours after discharge from hospital following the birth of the infant). Time trends also needed consideration. Some data were available on an annual basis (e.g. population estimates available from the Central Statistics Office) while other data were available only every three years (from the Programme for International Student Assessment study) or four years (from the Health Behaviours in School-Aged Children study). As the publication of the *State of the Nation's Children* was not aligned with these collection periods, the time period reported on referred to different time periods.

- *How the report should be compiled,* where issues related to the value of recognising the importance of taking a partnership approach with the multiple organisations who supplied the twenty-two data sources; balancing an ambition to produce the best-possible report while recognising the limitations of the data; acknowledging challenges and deficits arising; and presenting the data in a way that was accessible, unbiased and that did not compromise the credibility and value of the report.

Enablers when building an evidence base

While there were many challenges, there were also many enablers. Of these, the sponsorship and protection of the research programme by the Director General and senior policy-makers within the organisation was the most critical. The enabling impact of strong support by high-level leaders within the government structure who championed a changed approach and recognised, supported and vigorously promoted the use of evidence in decision-making cannot be underestimated. It also ensured that solutions to cross-government challenges could be addressed at a senior level by providing a mechanism to engage directly with high level policy-makers across government.

While the leadership of the organisation was the most beneficial aspect, other benefits also accrued from the Research Unit being embedded within a national policy-making structure and these are now considered.

Embeddedness within the national policy-making structure

Kano and Hayashi (2021) identify five core issues involved in the use of evidence in policy as methodological rigour, consistency, proximity, social appropriateness and legitimacy. In the case of developing and implementing this programme of research around children, proximity and legitimacy were critical. Being embedded within the national policy-making government department provided a mandate and opportunities that could never have been created or accessed from the outside.

The research unit that started in early 2003 in the National Children's Office, with a head of research and a single researcher, grew over the following nine years to include a statistician and two administrative personnel. Over the course of those years, formal and informal relationships, based on trust, mutual respect and mutual understandings, developed between those working in the research unit and those responsible for policy across different internal divisions and in other government departments. This was critical in getting agreement about key issues.

The head of research was a member of the senior management team at the Office of the Minister for Children and the Office of the Minister for Children and Youth Affairs, and this provided a platform for early engagement and mutual understandings of the activities and challenges faced by both policy-makers and researchers. Knowing about policies under development and other issues led to reciprocal exchanges of information on strategic developments. Implementation levers that emerged through the process of the development of the *National Strategy for Research and Data on Children's Lives* (such as the identification of needs, gaps, priorities and potential resources) could be promoted, embedded and, at times, recommended in other strategies and developments. The inclusion of a recommendation to develop a national research and data strategy in the 2006 partnership agreement, *Towards 2016*,[1] provided a platform and a clear policy imperative for the strategic development (Department of the Taoiseach 2006). The commitment to the generation, use and retrieval of evidence by those in charge meant that it was possible to be innovative and creative despite limited resources.

Leveraging the mandate

Working from within a government department meant that there was both the power and the credibility to access funding, create synergies and employ strategic and policy imperatives to support successful implementation of the programme. The embedded nature of the programme created an unambiguous mandate to seek out partnerships actively, and it also provided a platform and point of contact for other stakeholders seeking to progress their own research agendas. The power, credibility, mandate and platform were all critical in seeking and gaining assistance from stakeholders. In its absence, it would not have been possible to implement a strategic programme of research that engaged with so many stakeholders from so many different national and international organisations. Requests for assistance from a government department also provided a mandate to other organisations to progress developments that aligned with their own priorities.

The Health Research Board (HRB), for example, agreed to publish reports listing successful applications to the HRB funding schemes between 2000 and 2012 in the areas of infant/child health and infant/child mental health. The Central Statistics Office agreed in the 2011 Census of population to expand the age at which information was requested about caring responsibilities (from 15 years to 5 years), and in doing so provided a mechanism for identifying the prevalence of young carers. The three indicators that had

---

1   *Towards 2016*, which was published in 2006, was a Social Partnership Agreement between government and social partners. It presented a new framework to address key social challenges that the individual faces at each stage of life, and had a focus on the needs of children, young adults, people of working age, older people and people with disabilities.

been withdrawn from the Programme for International Student Assessment study survey in 2003 were reinstated in the Irish data collection in 2006 by the researchers at the Education Research Centre, in order to assist in reporting on the child wellbeing indicators. The researchers leading the *Health Behaviours in School-Aged Children* study agreed to include in their survey collection children aged 8–12 years, and this greatly enhanced the information available about the middle childhood period. These researchers also agreed to include in their survey a variable for children who identified as being from the Traveller community, and also children who identified as being disabled, thus enabling the disaggregation of data according to these characteristics in later *State of the Nation's Children* reports.

In summary, the mandate to develop better understandings of children facilitated and expedited the successful implementation of a number of strategic actions by other organisations. Sometimes these aligned and built on strategic decisions already under consideration by the organisations involved, but many, including those examples presented here, were agreed as a result of requests based on the identification of need, by the research unit.

Building strategic relationships

Although the National Children's Research Programme represented the first strategic approach to improving the understanding of children's lives, it is important to highlight that the landscape was not a blank canvas. There were many researchers and organisations already engaged in knowledge activities relevant to children's lives. These included, for example, the Central Statistics Office and the National Statistics Board who were engaged in a co-ordinated and strategic approach to building a sustainable data infrastructure. Activities such as the assessment of the statistical potential of administrative records (SPAR) (National Statistics Board 2003) and the development of formal data strategies within government departments acknowledged the importance of data in how policies were developed. Many researchers were investigating different aspects of children's lives, and international studies such as the *Health Behaviours in School-Aged Children* funded by the Department of Health and Children, the *Programme for International Student Assessment* study and ESPAD studies funded by the Department of Education and Skills, and the European Union Statistics on Income and Living Conditions (EU-SILC), focused on poverty across the EU and carried out by the Central Statistics Office, were already making a substantial contribution to the scientific body of knowledge about children's lives, as well as in concrete and meaningful ways. Findings from the *Programme for International Student Assessment* study, for example, provide comparative data on children's literacy, mathematics and science progress relative to their international peers, and directly inform education policy in Ireland. Data from the *Health Behaviours in School-Aged Children* continue to inform developments taking place in the Department of Health relating to children's physical activity levels and nutrition, as well as alcohol and drug use. Evidence from the EU-SILC study is used by organisations concerned with child poverty to bring attention and additional resources to children living in poverty.

The implementation of the NCS was built on a foundation that included organisational structures, funding and researchers that were already in place. As noted earlier, however, being embedded within a government organisation provided many opportunities for developing formal and informal relationships with stakeholders, and also for taking a co-ordinated approach to what was already in place. Every component of the research programme was implemented collaboratively in association with other stakeholders. A national and international Research and Information Advisory Panel, comprising national and international experts, which had provided guidance during the course of the NCS development, continued to provide assistance, particularly in reviewing and assessing applicants for the fellowship programme. The *Growing Up in Ireland* longitudinal study was commissioned in association with the Department of Social and Family Affairs and the Central Statistics Office, both of whom provided resources and support at every stage of the process.

From the outset, the research team within the department developed close working relationships with personnel at a strategic and operational level from the Central Statistics Office, and every substantive development around data (including the national set of child wellbeing indicators, the *State of the Nation's Children* reports and the *National Strategy for Research and Data on Children's Lives*) that took place included a representative from that organisation. This was also the case in respect of the personnel at the Health Promotion Research Centre, NUIG, where the principal investigator of the HBSC, Professor Saoirse NicGabhainn, was based. This relationship was particularly fruitful in terms of filling data and research gaps relating to children's health and in accessing research support. It was also successful in compiling the *State of the Nation's Children* reports, which were a collaborative effort between the research unit, statisticians from both the Department of Health and Children and Central Statistics Office, and researchers from the Health Promotion Research Centre, NUIG.

The *National Strategy for Research and Data on Children's Lives* development was overseen by a cross-departmental, multi-sectoral steering group, and a consultative and participative approach that involved extensive engagement with a range of stakeholders, including policy-makers, service-providers, researchers and children and young people, took place. These collaborations allowed for peer review as well as good governance, and also provided platforms for identifying challenges, obstacles and opportunities arising within their own and related organisations. Throughout, every opportunity was taken to engage with stakeholders at multiple levels in multiple organisations, and this promoted an understanding of the systematic and rigorous approach being adopted, thus giving legitimacy to the developments taking place. It also facilitated exchanges of information and allowed for developments and initiatives, as well as research and data requirements that had arisen to be addressed.

Adopting a systematic, evidenced and holistic approach to all developments

Each element of the Children's Research Programme was itself informed by a strong evidence base that had been developed systematically and scientifically. The availability of clear and unambiguous findings formed a compelling foundation for discussions with stakeholders across a range of areas and agencies when trying to develop better data and evidence. In addition, the broad conceptual underpinning of the Whole Child Perspective meant that every aspect of children's lives — their outcomes, the relationships around them, the formal and informal supports, and critically, children's own views on matters that affected them — was relevant to the implementation of the programme. This broad landscape provided a backdrop for the conditions and circumstances under which opportunities to improve understandings of children's lives could be identified and maximised. Each element of each development was written up in a transparent and comprehensive way, resulting in a number of reports and peer-review publications (Hanafin et al. 2007; Hanafin 2004; Clerkin et al. 2011; Hanafin 2014; Hanafin et al. 2013; Nic Gabhainn and Sixsmith 2006; Brooks et al. 2012; Brooks and Hanafin 2005; Roche, Hanafin and Sharek 2011).

A lot done and a lot more to do

The implementation of the strategic approach to research and data around children's lives was successful across a number of measures. By 2012, 28 studies including the *Growing Up in Ireland* longitudinal study of children, the largest study ever undertaken in respect of children in Ireland, had been commissioned. Following on from the implementation of the 2002–2012 programme, the *Growing Up in Ireland* longitudinal study has continued to be implemented, funded in part by the Atlantic Philanthropies, and there are now more than 80 reports based on the data from this study. Additional studies have also continued to be commissioned according to need and according to areas set out in the *National Strategy for Research and Data on Children's Lives*. More recent strategic developments have been aligned directly with specific policy documents such as the *Better Outcomes, Brighter Futures* (Department of Children and Youth Affairs 2014) document and *First 5: A Government Strategy for Babies, Young Children and their Families 2019–2028* (Department of Children and Youth Affairs 2018a).

Under the capacity-building programme, 40 Masters/PhD fellowships had been funded and 17 placements had been hosted in the OMCYA/DCYA by 2012. Several recipients of these awards have continued to undertake research in the area of children's lives, thus demonstrating the benefits of supporting researchers during their early careers. From 2011 to 2014, the capacity-building element of the programme supported specific research projects directly relevant to the outcome areas of the *National Strategy for Research and Data on Children's Lives*. A recent scheme referred to as the Department of Children and Youth Affairs / Irish Research Council Scholarship Scheme (2017–18) created funding for a PhD scholarship based on analysis of *Growing Up in Ireland* longitudinal study data and connected to the *Better Outcomes, Brighter Futures* policy (Department of Children and Youth Affairs 2014). In October 2018, another scholarship was authorised by the Department. The biennial *State of the Nation's Children Report* was published in 2016, and a revised National Set of Child Well-Being Indicators underpinned the 2020 publication (Department of Children and Youth Affairs 2020).

The process of development of the Irish national set of child wellbeing indicators was considered original, innovative and unique, particularly in incorporating children's viewpoints, and it was well received by policy-makers and academics internationally. Following publication, invitations were received by the authors from organisations such as UNICEF, the OECD and the EU Public Health Alliance, to present at international conferences and share our experiences. In addition, international publications such as the UNICEF report on child wellbeing in rich countries (UNICEF Office of Research 2013) incorporated many of the same indicators as had been identified in the national set of indicators, while a review of indicators across the OECD made a number of references to the Irish development (Bradshaw, Hoelscher and Richardson 2007).

The *State of the Nation's Children Report* signalled that children were important in the community and provided, in 2006, for the first time, an understanding of the wellbeing of children that was valid, reliable and comprehensive. Other benefits also accrued from the publication of *State of the Nation's Children*, including:

- Providing a mechanism for tracking changes over time
- Benchmarking progress across different groups and regions, nationally and internationally
- Highlighting policy issues arising
- Describing, monitoring and setting goals
- Assigning accountability, and
- Providing an impetus and focus for improvements in data about children's lives.

As far back as 2006, the UNCRC noted in its concluding comments:

> …the progress made with regard to the collection of statistical data, in particular the research functions of the National Children's Office within the National Children's Strategy, and the commissioned National Longitudinal Study on Children which will explore the lives of children in Ireland. (UNCRC 2006)

The *National Strategy for Research and Data on Children's Lives* provided leadership in understanding the lives of all children and had a particular focus on children with additional needs (Department of Children and Youth Affairs 2011; Hanafin et al. 2013). The co-ordinated approach, combined with the identification of priorities, minimised duplication of effort and maximised value for money. The systematic approach to building capacity had spin-offs in terms of access to funding, as well as the creation of a workforce fit for purpose in this area. The explicit commitment to the utilisation of research and data led to improved practices and policies, and through that, to improvements in children's lives. The final report on the implementation of the *National Strategy for Research and Data on Children's Lives* (Department of Children and Youth Affairs 2018b) noted that almost all actions had been implemented, and concluded:

> Thus the NSRDCL (National Strategy for Research and Data on Children's Lives) was a vital and significant development to drive forward research and data developments when it was initiated in 2011, and the implementation of key, ongoing and long-term initiatives and actions will continue to generate robust evidence to inform policy developments in respect of children and young people.

While there were a number of successes in improving understandings of children's lives, and several additional developments have taken place over the past number of years, many gaps in our knowledge about children remain. The *First 5* policy document identified several recommendations for research and data development where current understandings of children are limited. The revised set of child wellbeing indicators, aligned with the *Better Outcomes, Brighter Futures* policy document, highlighted a number of gaps where data were not available or available only infrequently. Challenges continue in what we know about children's health, in part due to a lack of electronic records and unique patient identifiers. Our knowledge about how best to protect and enhance children's lives through the virtual world needs to expand exponentially in order to mirror advancing digital developments.

More recent methodological developments in how data are collected — including, for example, through remote sensing passive personal monitors, GPS tracking of participants, mobile phones that are enhanced with applications and sensors, and the use of mobile applications to monitor noise and exposure to air pollutants — all provide entry points to understanding the interaction between children and the physical environment. Big Data, along with new analytic approaches, present possibilities for understanding children's lives well beyond our current capabilities, and this will require targeted capacity building in that area. Although the use of evidence in decision-making has been well problematised, novel and innovative solutions are relatively rare, and the importance of building and maintaining trusting and mutually respectful relationships can never be underestimated. Finally, it is suggested that embedding a dedicated research resource within policy organisations, with a leadership that values the use of evidence, brings with it the greatest possibility of getting the right evidence to the right person at the right time for the broadest number of issues.

References

Bradshaw, J., Hoelscher, P., and Richardson, D. (2007), 'Comparing Child Well-being in OECD Countries: Concepts and Methods', *Innocenti Working Paper,* no. 2006-03, Florence: UNICEF Innocenti Research Centre.

Bronfenbrenner, U. (1979), *The Ecology of Human Development*, Harvard MA : Harvard University Press.

Bronfenbrenner, U., and Morris, P.A. (1998), 'The Ecology of Developmental Processes', *Handbook of Child Psychology*, vol. 1, no. 5, pp 993–1028.

Brooks, A-M., and Hanafin, S. (2005), *Measuring Child Well-being: An Inventory of Key Indicators, Domains and Indicator Selection Criteria to Support the Development of a National Set of Child Well-being Indicators*, Dublin: Stationery Office.

Brooks, A-M., Geraghty, R., Fitzgerald, S., and Roche, G. (2012), Overview of inventory of data sources on children's lives.

Clerkin, P., Hanafin, S., Kelly, C., Gavin, A., de Róiste, A., and Nic Gabhainn, S. (2011), Cross-national case studies of children's data systems, Galway Health Promotion Research Centre, National University of Ireland, Galway.

Department of Children and Youth Affairs (2011), *The National Research and Data Strategy on Children's Lives 2011–2016*, Dublin: Department of Children and Youth Affairs.

Department of Children and Youth Affairs (2014), *Better Outcomes, Brighter Futures: The National Policy Framework for Children and Young People 2014–2020*, Dublin: Government Publications.

Department of Children and Youth Affairs (2018a), *First 5: A Whole-of-Government Strategy for Babies, Young Children and Their Families, 2019–2028*, Dublin: Government of Ireland.

Department of Children and Youth Affairs (2018b), *National Strategy for Research and Data on Children's Lives 2011–2016: Final Implementation*

Report, Action plan update to the end of 2016, Dublin: Department of Children and Youth Affairs.

Department of Children and Youth Affairs (2020), *State of the Nation's Children Report 2020*, Dublin: The Stationery Office.

Department of Health (2013), *Positive Ageing Starts Now! The National Positive Ageing Strategy*, Dublin: Department of Health.

Department of the Taoiseach (2006), *Towards 2016 – Ten-Year Framework Social Partnership Agreement 2006–2015*, Dublin: The Stationery Office.

Enterprise Ireland (2012), *Inventions & Innovations: The Positive Impact of Ideas from Research on Irish Industry and Society*, Dublin: Enterprise Ireland.

ESPAD Group (2020), *ESPAD Report 2019: Results from the European School Survey Project on Alcohol and Other Drugs*, Publications Office of the European Union, Luxembourg: EMCDDA Joint Publications.

Government of Ireland (2000), *The National Children's Strategy: Our Children – Their Lives*, November, Dublin: The Stationery Office. Available at untitled (earlychildhoodireland.ie)

Hanafin, S. (2004), *Review of Literature on the Delphi Technique*, Dublin: National Children's Office.

Hanafin, S. (2014), 'Impacts of Using Data to Report on Child Well-being', *CW365°*, available at https://cascw.umn.edu/wp-content/uploads/2014/04/CW360_Spring2014_WEB.pdf

Hanafin, S., and Brooks, A-M. (2009), 'From Rhetoric to Reality: Challenges in Using Data to Report on a National Set of Child Well-being Indicators', *Child Indicators Research*, vol. 2, no. 1, pp 33–55.

Hanafin, S., Brooks, A-M., Carroll, E., Fitzgerald, E., Nic Gabhainn, S., and Sixsmith, J. (2007), 'Achieving Consensus in Developing a National Set of Child Well-being Indicators', *Social Indicators Research*, vol. 80, no. 1, pp 79–104.

Hanafin, S., Roche, G., Brooks, A-M., Meaney, B. (2013), 'Evidence, Policy and Pragmatics: A Case Study on the Development of a National Research and Data Strategy on Children's Lives and the Role of Knowledge Exchange', *Evidence & Policy: A Journal of Research, Debate and Practice*, vol. 9, no. 1, pp 29–42.

Hasen, R.L. (2019), 'Deep Fakes, Bots, and Siloed Justices: American Election Law in a Post-Truth World', *St Louis University Law Journal*.

Health Research Board (2016), *HRB Strategy 2016–2020*, Dublin: National Statistics Board.

Hibell, B., Andersson, B., Ahlström, S., Balakireva, O., Bjarnason, T., Kokkevi, A., et al. (2000), *The 1999 ESPAD report: Alcohol and Other Drug Use Among Students in 30 European Countries*, Swedish Council for Information on Alcohol and Other Drugs, p. 26.

Higgins, K. (2016), 'Post-Truth: A Guide for the Perplexed', *Nature*, vol. 540, no. 7631: 9.

Kano, H., and Hayashi, T.I. (2021), 'A Framework for Implementing Evidence in Policymaking: Perspectives and Phases of Evidence Evaluation in the Science–Policy Interaction', *Environmental Science & Policy*, vol. 116, pp 86–95.

Kaoukji, D. and Little, M. (2007), 'Interview with Sylda Langford: People, Relationships and Power Struggles – The View from the Director-General of the Irish Office of the Minister for Children', *Journal of Children's Services*, vol. 2, no. 1, pp 67–75.

Langford, S. (2007), 'Delivering Integrated Policy and Services for Children', *Journal of the Statistical and Social Inquiry Society of Ireland*, vol. 36, June, pp 205–60.

Lee, D., Cyganiak, R. and Decker, S. (2014), *Open Data Ireland: Open Data Publication Handbook*, Galway: Insight Centre for Data Analytics, NUI Galway.

Murphy, D., Williams, J., Murray, A., and Smyth, E. (2019), *Growing up in Ireland: Design, Instrumentation and Procedures for Cohort '98 at 17/18 Years of Age*, Dublin: Department of Children and Youth Affairs.

National Competitiveness Council (2015), *Ireland's Competitiveness Challenge 2015*, Dublin: National Competitiveness Council.

National Statistics Board (2003), *Statistical Potential of Administrative Records: An Examination of Data Holdings in Six Government Departments*, Working Report, Dublin: National Statistics Board.

National Statistics Board (2015), *A World Class Statistical System for Ireland 2015–2020*, Dublin: National Statistics Board.

Nic Gabhainn, S., and Sixsmith, J. (2006), 'Children Photographing Well-being: Facilitating Participation in Research', *Children & Society*, vol. 20, no. 4, pp 249–59.

Office of the Minister for Children (OMC) (2006), *State of the Nation's Children Ireland 2006*, Dublin: The Stationery Office.

Office of the Minister for Children and Youth Affairs (OMCYA) (2008), *State of the Nation's Children Report 2008*, Dublin: The Stationery Office.

Office of the Minister for Children and Youth Affairs (OMCYA) (2010), *State of the Nation's Children Report 2010*, Dublin: The Stationery Office.

Oliver K.A., and de Vocht F. (2017), 'Defining "Evidence" in Public Health: A Survey of Policymakers' Uses and Preferences', *European Journal of Public Health*, vol. 27 (suppl_2), pp 112–7.

Roche, G., Hanafin, S., and Sharek, D. (2011), *Report on Public Consultation Processes for National Strategy for Research and Data on Children's Lives 2011–2016*, Dublin: Department of Children and Youth Affairs. Available at: www. dcya. ie

Science Foundation Ireland (2012), *Agenda 2020: Excellence and Impact*, Dublin: Science Foundation Ireland.

Shaxson, L. (2005), 'Is Your Evidence Robust Enough? Questions for Policy Makers and Practitioners', *Evidence & Policy: A Journal of Research, Debate and Practice*, vol. 1, no. 1, pp 101–12.

United Nations Committee on the Rights of the Child (UNCRC) (1998), Concluding observations of the Committee on the Rights of the Child: Ireland.

United Nations Committee on the Rights of the Child (UNCRC) (2006), Consideration of reports submitted by states parties under Article 44 on the Convention on the Rights of the Child: Concluding observations: Ireland.

UNICEF Office of Research (2013), 'Child Well-being in Rich Countries: A Comparative Overview', *Innocenti Report Card* 11, Florence: UNICEF Office of Research.

CHAPTER 3

CHILDCARE[1] POLICY DEVELOPMENT IN IRELAND: THE CASE OF EARLY CHILDHOOD EDUCATION AND CARE

Nóirín Hayes

Introduction

Retrospective reviews of the contribution of policy-makers often seek out patterns and connections to create a linear narrative of cause and effect, even as they point to the power of the unknown or the whim of external events. In reviewing the trajectory of policy in early childhood education and care (ECEC) under the leadership of Sylda Langford, there is in fact a linear narrative that is evident in her strategic, responsive approaches to unexpected challenges and opportunities. It unfolds as the story of a pragmatic negotiator with a long-term vision, who has navigated a bumpy road and consciously laid a foundation for policy that has yet to be leveraged to full effect.

Her influence has been far-reaching in many fields across equality, child and youth policy, and she has been a seminal influence in childcare policy-

---

1   Childcare refers to two distinct service types: Early Childhood Education and Care (ECEC) services for children from birth to 6 years of age (compulsory school age in Ireland) and School Age Childcare for school-going children. In the main, this chapter refers to ECEC.

making and development. Over the period of her involvement, investment in the ECEC system grew, awareness about the unique nature and importance of the sector was strengthened, and key infrastructural elements upon which to build a strong and sustainable system were commenced. The extensive and systemic nature of this impact has made structuring this chapter a challenge. For simplicity, I have divided it broadly into three five-year periods: 1995–2000, 2000-2005 and 2005–2010.

1995–2000

It was during the final decade of the last century that a series of factors came together to create a climate for significant policy action on childcare, one informed by a recognition of the importance of childcare as a policy focus and of the potential of the opportunities presented. The challenges were many, including the fact that at least six departments were involved to some degree in the support, funding or regulation of childcare (Hayes 1995).

Irish legislation in respect of children has tended to be protectionist in nature, aiming to protect children within the family context. The 1908 Children's Act was the dominant legislative instrument relating to children throughout the twentieth century, although principles of practice and policy had evolved and changed considerably over that time. It was not until 1991 that the Child Care Act replaced elements of the 1908 Act. The Child Care Act, 1991 marked a significant shift in attention to children and children's services in Ireland and outlined the role of the State in the promotion of the welfare of children and the provision of family support services. Section VII of the Child Care Act, 1991 gave a new and wider responsibility to the State in the regulation and supervision of pre-school services for all children, rather than restricting regulation to services developed for children considered 'at risk'. For a variety of reasons, the enabling of Section VII was not commenced until 1996 through the Child Care (Pre-School Services) Regulations.

In addition to national factors converging to drive policy developments on childcare, international influences also played a significant role. These included a commitment to expanding and developing certain children's services, which became urgent following a critical report from the UN Committee on the Rights of the Child, arising from the first plenary hearing of the Irish National Report on realising the UN Convention on the Rights of the Child in Irish policy and practice (Langford 2007). Specifically, the UN Committee recommended that '…the State party adopt a comprehensive

National Strategy for Children, incorporating the principles and provisions of the Convention' (Children's Rights Alliance, 1998). In October 1998, at a Children's Rights Alliance (CRA) conference held to mark the UN Committee report, the then Minister for Health and Children, Brian Cowen TD, announced the Government's commitment to act on the UN Committee's recommendation to develop a national children's strategy. The Strategy, *Our Children – Their Lives* (Ireland, 2000a) laid the foundation for child policy in Ireland for ten years, including childcare policy, noting that '[C]hildren's early education and developmental needs will be met through quality childcare services and family-friendly employment measures' (p. 50).

This strategy also led to the establishment of the National Children's Office (NCO), designated a key role in drawing together different departments on complex cross-cutting issues, with a view to developing and implementing integrated policy and providing national leadership in the context of meeting local needs. However, despite its potential, 'A weakness of the National Children's Office was its inability to influence mainstream departments. It did not have the power or the authority' (Kaoukji and Little 2007, p. 69).

Developments in Europe were also becoming influential. Under its equality agenda, the EU was making funding available for equality initiatives, some focusing on childcare as a barrier for women's equal access to the labour market. These initiatives coincided with the work of the European Childcare Network, which highlighted, among other things, the very low level of state support for childcare in Ireland when compared to other European countries (European Commission Network on Childcare 1996). By the 1990s, the impact of national and international reports, recommendations from different working groups and the availability of European funding created opportunities for policy action in relation to childcare, opportunities recognised by the Department of Justice, Equality and Law Reform (DJELR).

National Childcare Strategy (2000–2006)

The availability of childcare as a wide-ranging equality issue of relevance to both men and women was recognised by Sylda Langford in her evidence to an Oireachtas Committee that 'There will never be equality in Ireland until it is seen as a men's issue and men and women share work and domestic roles equally' (Pollak 1999). When the DJELR moved to develop a National Childcare Strategy towards integrating the different strands of the current policy arrangements for childcare and early educational services, she was well placed to take a key role.

To move towards the development of a childcare infrastructure, an Expert Working Group (EWG) was established and chaired by the DJELR. Committing to the 'spirit' of the *Partnership 2000*[2] (Government of Ireland 1996) the work of the EWG emphasised shared understanding, interdependence between the partners, and support and commitment through using a problem-solving approach. *Partnership 2000* had called for the development of a national childcare framework. However, under the guidance of the chair, the remit was altered to developing a national childcare strategy. The decision to move from a 'framework' to a 'strategy' was a tactical one as the term 'framework' could be interpreted as, and limited to, considering delivery mechanisms only.

In determining membership of the EWG it was agreed to make it as inclusive as possible, representing all the stakeholders with an interest in the development of childcare. This method was adopted to bring together what was a fragmented selection of interested parties with different ambitions and aspirations. It was a prudent approach, intended to ensure the development of a comprehensive national strategy, which would meet the needs of all children and parents and take into account the views of as many childcare interests as possible. The eighty members represented social partners, statutory bodies, non-governmental organisations, parents' groups and the relevant government departments. This latter reflected an understanding of the importance of cross-departmental engagement and, in particular, the key role of the Department of Health (inspection) and the Department of Education and Science (quality and curriculum). The large membership of the group required strong and confident leadership, together with careful design and structure. It operated at three levels:

- Plenary sessions attended by all members
- Eight sub-groups, each focusing on a particular policy issue
- A Steering Group.

As Chair of the Early Education sub-group, I was also a member of the Steering Group. I was impressed by the even-handed but nonetheless rigorous style of Sylda as Chair. She had a clear focus for the group and awareness of some of its limitations, she was prepared to listen to dissenting voices but managed to get consensus and, where a problem arose, she was

---

2   Aimed at ensuring industrial stability, the 'partnership' approach was guided by, among other things, the emerging potential of EU funding to support farming and contribute to combating disadvantage and promoting equality.

willing to give time to resolve it. As Chair, she was ambitious for the strategy but also sensitive to the financial and cultural realities of the time.

The final, agreed, report of the EWG proposed a comprehensive, seven-year National Childcare Strategy (NCS) (Government of Ireland 1999) for the management and development of the childcare sector. The strategy represented the first concerted attempt to develop a coherent and comprehensive government policy that specifically addressed childcare. The terms of reference were to consider childcare in respect of children whose parent/s were either at work or attempting to access work through training and/or education. This limitation reflects a weakness in the strategy, resulting in provisions under the NCS being inextricably linked to labour-market participation, rather than taking a broader view of childcare (Hayes 2002). It could also be considered ironic given that childcare policies have been hampered by an underlying tension between the ideology of the traditional family and the economic necessity for women to work (Hayes 2001). Reflecting the skill of the Chair at keeping doors of opportunity ajar, the NCS stated that '...improving the quality and quantity of childcare will also have a positive effect on parents who choose to care for their child at home since 16% of children with parents who work full-time in the home avail of paid childcare' (DJELR 1999, p. xxv).

A significant source of funding for the strategy was channelled through the *National Development Plan 2000–2006* (Government of Ireland 2000b). The National Development Plan (NDP) directed funding and support to the development of early education and early intervention towards improving long-term education participation. It also identified childcare as a key aspect of the social-inclusion agenda, where the primary objective of childcare was seen as overcoming social disadvantage and promoting equality by improving access to education, training and work and reconciling work and family life. Through accessing significant European funding, these ambitions were managed and funds distributed under the Equal Opportunities Childcare Programme (EOCP) 2000–2006.

2000–2005

For the childcare system and those working within it, the period 2000–2005 could be said to have been the 'golden age'. There was extensive policy development, substantial funding and a general sense that a clear path towards a sustainable childcare sector for children, parents and staff was emerging. The EOCP is one of the most important developments in the support and development of ECEC and was the primary source of funding available to existing childcare providers as well as those seeking to develop new childcare facilities. At the same time as the NCS was published, the Department of Education and Science published a White Paper on Early Childhood Education, *Ready to Learn* (Department of Education and Science 1999). This publication led to the establishment, in 2002, of the Centre for Early Childhood Development and Education (CECDE), a centre that worked closely with, and was supported by, the DJELR in many aspects of ECEC policy, particularly on issues of quality practice (CECDE 2006) and research. Another important development followed on from the publication of the Education Act, 1998. As a consequence of this Act, the National Council for Curriculum and Assessment (NCCA) became responsible for the development of a curriculum framework for early childhood services (NCCA 2009). These intertwined developments all fed into the overall vision for ECEC.

Equal Opportunities Childcare Programme (EOCP)

Supported by substantial EU funding and linked to the *Partnership 2000* commitment to resource measures to develop the childcare sector, the Equal Opportunities Childcare Programme (EOCP) was introduced as an employment-equality measure, designed to encourage more women to enter the workforce. The opportunities provided were extensive and leveraged to extremely useful effect to highlight that the childcare programme also served other social policy goals, such as ensuring the wellbeing and early development of all young children, particularly those from disadvantaged families.

The primary aim of the EOCP was accompanied by three objectives: to enhance the quality of childcare, to increase the number of childcare facilities and childcare places, and to introduce a co-ordinated approach to the delivery of childcare services. While developing services and infrastructure to meet the needs of a diverse range of parents, particularly those trying to reconcile work and family life, the EOCP was also committed to ensuring that the needs of the child were paramount.

During this period, several funding schemes and structures were established to support the implementation of the programme and the development of the emergent childcare sector more generally. Funds were accessed to support capital and staffing grants. Capital grants were available to community/not-for-profit organisations and self-employed and private childcare providers towards the cost of building, renovation, upgrading or equipping childcare facilities. Staffing grants were provided to community/not-for-profit organisations towards the cost of staff for community-based provision in disadvantaged areas. Under this scheme, several Area-Based Partnerships and community groups were supported to develop innovative early education and childcare projects. These programmes were the forerunner to the current Area Based Childhood (ABC) programmes co-ordinated through Tusla – The Child and Family Agency (www.tusla.ie).

Reflecting a belief that leadership and organisation are essential to facilitate effective integration and cross-departmental collaboration, Sylda created a number of different oversight and advisory groups, including a Childcare Directorate within the DJELR, a National Co-ordinating Childcare Committee (NCCC) and 33 County/City Childcare Committees.

The Childcare Directorate

The Childcare Directorate was located within the Equality Division of the DJELR and was responsible for the EOCP. The Directorate also engaged in interdepartmental policy work on issues relating to the childcare sector, such as regulation, the then responsibility of the Department of Health and Children (now Tusla) and early education, which was a matter for the Department of Education and Science. Conscious of the significance of integrated ECEC policy development, which valued care and education equally, efforts continued to facilitate structural integration at departmental level. However, it was clear that integrated policy development 'would take time to establish and would be incremental in approach given that responsibility for areas relating to children's policy and services was spread across Government Departments and agencies' (Langford 2006).

The Directorate proved very successful in its remit and has been significantly strengthened over time, reflecting its central role in childcare policy. It continues to function today in an extended form within the Department of Children, Equality, Diversity, Integration and Youth (DCEDIY).

The National Co-ordination Childcare Committee (NCCC)

The NCCC was established as an advisory body to oversee the co-ordinated development of an integrated childcare infrastructure. It had wide-ranging, cross-sectoral representation with technical and financial assistance from Area Development Management (ADM).[3] As a co-ordinating committee,

---

3   ADM was established in 1992 in an agreement between the Irish Government and the European Commission to manage EU grants for local development. It provided technical assistance and financial management to the EOCP.

rather than a management board, its influence was limited, and this created difficulties in supporting and monitoring the quality of services and local policy developments, which led to unnecessary duplication in developments of, for instance, protocols and resources (Hayes 2002). Nonetheless, the NCCC was an important and inclusive forum for discussion and planning aspects of EOCP implementation and management.

Under the NCCC, several sub-groups were formed, and the work of some of these groups had significant impact on the ECEC system and continues to be influential today. For instance, the Advisory Group on Equality and Diversity developed the *Diversity and Equality Guidelines for Childcare Providers* (Office of the Minister for Children 2006), which were subsequently updated to the *Diversity, Equality and Inclusion Charter and Guidelines for Early Childhood Care and Education* (Department of Children and Youth Affairs 2016). The Certifying Body Sub-group developed a draft framework to address qualification, accreditation and certification issues (DJELR 2002) which laid the foundation for the Workforce Development initiatives that continue today.

County/City Childcare Committees (CCCs)

The EOCP supported the establishment of 33 County/City Childcare Committees (CCCs) to promote, develop and support high-quality childcare at a local level. It is through the CCCs that much of the infrastructure necessary to support childcare has been developed and delivered. Over time, their remit has evolved to take account of other developments and opportunities within the childcare system. They now offer an extensive support service at local level, including advice on setting up a childcare business; childcare information sessions; training courses; advice and support on applying for government funding; and services to parents, such as providing information on local childcare facilities and on parent networks. They remain one of the most important and effective childcare structures developed.

While many of the initiatives aimed at enhancing the quality of childcare services were being developed co-operatively with the Departments of Health, Children, and Education and Science, the DJELR was directly supporting some under the EOCP. As noted, '[O]n the "supply-side", the Government's approach has been to stimulate the provision of quality childcare places, through the provision of grants for the childcare sector' (Langford 2007, p. 259). These grants were intended to strengthen what was a weak system and included financial support to the National Voluntary Childcare Organisations[4] charged with implementing a range of measures aimed at upskilling their members and creating a greater and better-informed awareness of quality in relation to childcare. This group continues to exist today in the form of the National Childcare Voluntary Collaborative and is active in engaging with the various policy developments under the DCEDIY. A testament to the foresight and understanding of the challenges and potential of the childcare sector is evident in the continued existence of so many of the structures established under the EOCP.

2005–2010

The investment in, and the direction of, childcare policy in Ireland moved childcare out from the shadows into mainstream public attention. Childcare places were growing, training opportunities expanding, and research was consolidating. However, certain difficulties continued to provide challenges. The growth of services, mainly private, outpaced the measures to ensure the quality of services, and children's experiences of ECEC varied widely. In addition, the costs of childcare to parents continued to rise. The situation was exacerbated by a shift in policy focus following the financial crisis of 2008 and the subsequent recession. During this dynamic and difficult period, the NCO continued to seek increased funding and support to grow a high-quality childcare system. The challenges were, however, formidable.

From NCO to OMC

The establishment of the Office of the Minister for Children (OMC) marks one of the greatest and most influential achievements of this period. Two major influencing factors in the formation of the OMC have been identified. The first went back to the establishment of the NCO which was responsible for driving policy for children's issues across all government departments. Although with limited authority the NCO did develop the concept of participation and consultation with children in Ireland, it focused on research and encouraged the practice of evidence-based policy-making. It also

> …signalled a recognition of the fact that children's issues were emerging as a specific area of policy and high-level goals. Its

---

4   This group currently comprises Barnardos, Childminding Ireland, Early Childhood Ireland, Irish Steiner Kindergarten Association, National Childhood Network, National Parents Council and St Nicholas Montessori Teachers Association/Society of Ireland.

> integration into the OMC provides a further dimension and
> direction to the Office as we go forward…. (Langford 2006, p. 67)

The second factor came from the DJELR itself, where a change in strategic focus provided a unique opportunity to undertake a review of these services, which

> …used a task force rather than an inter-departmental group
> because in my experience it was important to deal with power
> sharing and the sharing of responsibilities…. The evidence …
> was that the best outcomes were achieved where agencies were
> brought together under the direction of one body, so long as
> the policy and practice emerging from the single body were
> properly funded. (Kaoukji and Little 2007, p. 69)

The timing was opportune for raising the possibility of a designated office as outlined below:

> Presenting to a Cabinet sub-committee instead of sending a
> memo straight to Cabinet provides the opportunity to argue the
> case, to be open to questions from ministers, to articulate current
> weaknesses in services and to be able to argue what should be
> done to address those weaknesses. Because these discussions
> took place just before the annual budget, the outcome of the
> discussions became subject to rules surrounding budget secrecy
> and this helped in the delivery of the Government's decision.
> (ibid, p. 69).

The OMC was established in December 2005 (becoming the Office of the Minister for Children and Youth Affairs [OMCYA] in 2008), and was responsible for policy work in childcare, children's services and youth justice, while responsibility for service delivery remained with the departments. It brought this series of functions under a single Minister with delegated responsibilities across the Departments of Justice, Education and Health. Although a Junior Minister of State, the Minister for Children attended Cabinet meetings, an important step forward in bringing a visibility to children and their affairs that was previously absent. The OMC was responsible for interacting with every department and every agency that could contribute to policy leading to better outcomes for children. The challenges this presented were significant, but the OMC was committed to improving the wellbeing of children and anxious to drive the implementation of those ideas. As a model of integrated policy in action, the OMC was a space where government departments and agencies could work together with an onus on departments to co-operate rather than compete.

Given the extensive remit of the OMCYA, it is not possible to do justice to its influences. For the purposes of this chapter, I have selected two examples to illustrate how its approach has had, and continues to have, a critical influence on ECEC policy into the present.

Universal Free Preschool Years

The ability to respond to opportunities to move policy in a particular direction can be seen in the history and introduction in 2010 of the universal Free Preschool Year. In a 2007 interview, Sylda noted that her modus operandi included:

> …keeping an eye on the aspirations of political parties as a national election beckons. But my task is not just the orthodox one of anticipating what these will mean for the single department in which I work; rather it is also the unorthodox one of anticipating what it will mean for the three Departments of Health, Education and Justice that surround the OMC. For example, nearly all of the political parties are making commitments in relation to having universal pre-school in place by a certain time but they advocate different funding mechanisms. This allows me to do some preparatory work, for example looking at how much pre-school provision exists in the country. (Kaoukji and Little 2007, p. 72)

Such a forward-thinking, preparatory approach formed the basis of a bold action when the opportunity arose, as it did in respect of ECEC.

To address continued concerns about the cost of ECEC to parents, the Government, in 2006, introduced an Early Childcare Supplement (ECS) for all parents of children under 6 years of age. This was a direct, non-taxable payment in respect of each eligible child, at a cost to the State, on commencement, of €350m annually. While the ECS was designed to assist all parents of children under 6 years in covering their ECEC costs, there was no obligation for parents to spend the money on ECEC, and the scheme was not designed to strengthen the ECEC sector, support staff or improve and sustain quality. Following the 2008 financial crisis, the Irish Government sought to reduce spending significantly across the board. Measures included reducing the relatively new ECS, and in its 2009 budget statement the Government announced that while it was moving to abolish the ECS, an element of the funding would be ring-fenced to provide a universal Free Preschool Year (FPSY) for all children aged between 3 years 3 months and 4 years 7 months. This change in policy direction was unexpected but welcome, as it was in keeping with calls from many individuals and policy bodies over the years. It is difficult not to imagine that strategic forward planning played a significant part in guiding thinking in this direction.

The FPSY scheme brought Irish ECEC policy more closely in line with international developments and marked the first time that investment was clearly directed at the services themselves. Although insufficiently funded, the move has had a profound impact on the ECEC system in Ireland, leading to investment in quality supports for the programme, and incentives to encourage more qualified staff to work within the scheme, thus enhancing the overall profile of staff working in ECEC. It has also led to an enhanced awareness of the crucial role ECEC plays in the lives of children and their families.

Philanthropy and Prevention and Early Intervention (PEI)

A second example of the value of foresight and responsiveness to opportunities can be seen in the engagement of the OMC with philanthropy and the development of a partnership on policy development and service delivery. Atlantic Philanthropies established in Ireland in 1987 but turned its attention to children and youth only in 2003 (Boyle 2016). Through working in partnership with government, they aimed to support the development of services directly, while supporting it indirectly through influencing policy. Recognising the transformative potential significant funding could have on services in areas of disadvantage, but also sensitive to the tensions of partnering with philanthropy, Sylda noted in a 2007 interview that working with philanthropy:

> …is exciting but it also represents an act of faith that the sites will be able to implement, evaluate and mainstream their most effective services, that we will be able to keep the best

of all existing services going and that we will be able to learn sufficient to mainstream some combination of the two…. (Kaoukji and Little 2007, p. 72)

Such thinking laid the foundation for what became known as the Programme for Early Intervention (PEI). The long-term objective for investment was to support programmes that would have a sustained impact

> …on the communities involved, the monitoring and evaluation of the projects will present the OMC with an opportunity to learn about 'what works' in the field and to transfer that learning to mainstream service provision. (Ibid, p. 72)

Recognising the challenge this presented, Sylda made a particularly prescient observation that:

> …many excellent initiatives have remained at the 'pilot' stage for years due to a lack of focus on transferring the learning to the mainstream services. Therefore, in my view, planning for the transfer of learning needs to commence as soon as possible in the lifespan of the Programme. (Ibid, p. 72)

To facilitate the transfer of learning and build a knowledge base that could be used into the future, a central requirement of funding under the PEI was that all programmes supported would be rigorously evaluated. This was stipulated to generate national evidence that could be used to inform subsequent policy.

Investments under the partnership of the OMC and philanthropy led to the design of innovative programmes to support children and their families. The ambitions of the PEI were, however, curtailed following the financial crisis of 2008 and the subsequent recession. The accelerated shift in policy that resulted from the recession led to a situation where programmes have remained at a relatively 'pilot' stage and the mainstream has not been changed as significantly as envisioned. However, the vision, principles and foundations that were laid for evidence-gathering and transfer of learning were strong and continue to inform present-day policy. Some of the initial programmes continue to flourish, as do structures such as the Prevention and Early Intervention Network (https://www.pein.ie), the Area Based

Childhood initiatives and the WhatWorks learning/sharing hub (https://whatworks.gov.ie).

Conclusion

An understanding of the subtleties of policy language is critical to effective policy formation, and its power is revealing. It is, for instance, evident in the decision to develop a National Childcare Strategy rather than a 'framework' as originally recommended. Similarly, when presented with the possibility of chairing an interdepartmental group on youth justice, the opportunity was taken to create a task force and leverage the power that brought. Among the most significant challenges Sylda identified for the OMC was:

> ...a psychological one. In Ireland the OMC is the first joined-up piece of Government executive, so we are acting as a role model for potential future connections. In the past, once a civil servant like me moved outside their primary policy area they became a voice in the wilderness. (Kaoukji and Little 2007, p. 72)

As we enter a period where there are increased calls for a reimagining of the ECEC sector that meets the rights and needs of children (INFORM 2020) and a new model of childcare that is flexible and inclusive of all children (Programme for Government 2020), and where the challenges of affordability and accessibility remain, we do not have to start from the beginning. The backbone of a high-quality, stable and sustainable model of integrated ECEC has been established. It includes local structures such as the CCCs and NVCOs, the national quality, curricular and diversity frameworks and structures addressing the qualifications and professional status of ECEC staff. In strengthening ECEC into the future, there is a strong foundation on which to build.

References

Boyle, R. (2016), *Philanthropy Working with Government: A Case Study of the Atlantic Phialanthropies' Partnership with the Irish Government*, Dublin: IPA.

Centre for Early Childhood Development and Education (CECDE) (2006), *Síolta: The National Quality Framework for Early Childhood Education*, Dublin: CECDE.

Children's Rights Alliance (CRA) (1998), *CRA Newsletter*, issue 8, Dublin: CRA.

Department of Children and Youth Affairs (DCYA) (2016), *Diversity, Equality and Inclusion Charter and Guidelines for Early Childhood Care and Education*, Dublin: DCYA.

Department of Education and Science, *Ready to Learn: White Paper on Early Education*, Dublin: The Stationery Office.

Department of Justice, Equality and Law Reform (1999), *National Childcare Strategy: Report of the Partnership 2000 Expert Working Group on Childcare*, Dublin: The Stationery Office. Available at Childcare1.pdf (justice.ie)

Department of Justice, Equality and Law Reform (2002), *Model Framework for Education, Training and Professional Development in the Early Childhood Care and Education Sector*, Dublin: The Stationery Office.

European Commission Network on Childcare (1996), *A Review of Services for Young Children in the European Union, 1990–1995*, London: EC Network on Childcare.

Government of Ireland (1996), *Partnership 2000 for Inclusion, Employment and Competitiveness*, Dublin: The Stationery Office.

Government of Ireland (1999), *National Childcare Strategy: Report of the Partnership 2000 Expert Working Group on Childcare*, Dublin: The Stationery Office.

Government of Ireland (2000a), *The National Children's Strategy: Our Children – Their Lives*, November, Dublin: Government Publications. Available at untitled (earlychildhoodireland.ie).

Government of Ireland (2000b), *National Development Plan*, Dublin: The Stationery Office.

Hayes, N. (1995), *The Case for a National Policy on Early Education*, Poverty and Policy discussion paper No. 2, Dublin: Combat Poverty Agency.

Hayes, N. (2001), 'Early Childhood Education in Ireland', *Administration*, vol. 49, no. 3, pp 43–67.

Hayes, N. (2002), *Children's Rights – Whose Right? A Review of Child Policy Development in Ireland: Studies in Public Policy 9*, Dublin: Trinity College Dublin Policy Institute.

INFORM (2020), *Act Now: Re-imagining Early Childhood Education and Care*, Dublin: INFORM.

Kaoukji, D. and Little, M. (2007), 'Interview with Sylda Langford: People, Relationships and Power Struggles – The View from the Director-General of the Irish Office of the Minister for Children', *Journal of Children's Services*, vol. 2, issue 1, pp 67–75.

Langford, S. (2006), 'The Development of Childcare Policy in Ireland During 1996–2006' in Hayes, N., and Bradley, S., *A Decade of Reflection: Early Childhood Care and Education in Ireland: 1996–2006*, Dublin: CSER/DIT, pp 65–9.

Langford, S. (2007), 'Delivering Integrated Services and Policies for Children', *Journal of the Statistical and Social Inquiry Society of Ireland*, vol. XXXVI, pp 250–60.

National Council for Curriculum and Assessment (NCCA) (2009), *Aistear – The Early Childhood Curriculum Framework*, Dublin: NCCA.

Office of the Minister for Children (OMC) (2006), *Diversity and Equality Guidelines for Childcare Providers*, Dublin: Government Publications.

Pollak, A. (1999), 'Equality an issue for men also – Justice official', *The Irish Times*, 16 July.

Programme for Government (2020), *Our Shared Future*, Dublin: The Stationery Office.

PART II

Putting Policy into Practice – Reaching the Most Vulnerable

CHAPTER 4

Challenges Facing the Development of Child-Protection and Welfare Services for Children in Ireland Today: Reclaiming Good Ethical Practice

Cormac Quinlan

Introduction

This chapter explores the central importance of social work values and ethics to its core foundation in relationship-based practice, the influence of our current child protection and welfare system on this practice, and key changes required to both the system and to practice to ensure that these essential ethical practices remain central to the children, families and communities we serve.

Every day we come across heartrending stories of harm to children. We see or hear the impact of domestic violence, homelessness, abuse and neglect on children, and we find it almost impossible to believe or understand how individuals can act in a way that might knowingly seek to place a vulnerable child in danger. Yet we also recognise that growing unemployment, housing shortages, poverty and increased pressure on parents and families have led many to struggle to make ends meet, to fall into substance or alcohol misuse or to find themselves pushed to the end of their tether to sustain a safe and supportive environment for themselves and their children. We also hear the horrific accounts from survivors of abuse, of the hurt and trauma they experienced at the hands of their abuser or indeed a society that failed to protect them.

Social workers operate in this world on a daily basis. We are asked, indeed required, to step into a world full of inequality, incredibly complex problems, significant hurt and trauma, and we are asked to make a difference. In doing so, we are typically expected to balance rights and navigate the space between private family life and the role the State plays in protecting children, always making sure that we intervene in a way that protects a child but does not destroy the integrity of normal family life. Navigating such spaces undoubtedly requires expert knowledge and skill, but perhaps more importantly, it requires a critical awareness and ability to walk this fine line and be guided by a core set of values and ethics. Without a set of guiding principles to provide us with a moral direction, it would be impossible for us to achieve our complex balancing task, whether that involves intervening in an individual child's life or, indeed, advocating and promoting social change. However, holding on to our values in a climate driven by fear, anxiety and the impact of ever-increasing accountability is not an easy task. Social work practice and the wider system surrounding this practice remain critically dependent on each other in continuously shaping an evolving child-protection and welfare system.

The importance of social work values and ethics

Social Work is a practice-based profession and an academic discipline that promotes social change and development, social cohesion, and the empowerment and liberation of people. Principles of social justice, human rights, collective responsibility and respect for diversities are central to social work. (International Federation of Social Workers 2014)

Social work recognises the unique value of each human being and it seeks to connect or, indeed, reconnect the person to other people, resources and supports that can allow them to live meaningful and fulfilled lives. In doing so, it values the power of human connectivity and the essential nature of human relationships, and therefore utilises, most of all, relationship-based practice. Ingram and Smith (2018) highlight the key points emerging from literature on the centrality of relationship to social work and conclude by stating that social work relationships are 'arguably, the defining characteristic of the profession'. In social work there is a belief that if most of society's problems are relational then relationships also hold the key to solutions. The stronger the bonds or networks someone has, then the better they are able to face life's challenges. As far back as the 1950s, Biestek (1957) had described the appropriate attitudes, knowledge and abilities required of a social worker in their casework relationship and set them out in the context of their being ethical principles. These principles become the foundation of a commonly shared understanding of how we should act and behave in our professional role – an understanding that has continued to the present day. These are the rules that govern the expected behaviour of the person as established by the collective professional group.

The increased recognition of social work as a distinct, protected and thus regulated profession in Ireland has most recently been endorsed by inclusion of social work as one of the regulated professions under the Health and Social Care Professionals Act, 2005. Social work became the first profession under this new legislation to see both the title of social work to be protected in law and for high public standards to apply to social work practice to ensure the protection of the public. The core and shared values to which the profession now collectively holds itself to account are its Code of Professional Conduct and Ethics (CORU 2019). As CORU states on its website:

> The Code sets out the standard of conduct, performance and ethics which a member of that profession must adhere to throughout the course of their work.

For illustrative purposes, I have adapted and selected core elements of the International Federation of Social Work's *Global Social Work Statement of Ethical Principles* (July 2018) and given brief consideration of them in respect of some of the expectations they place on social workers within child protection and welfare practice. These principles are also endorsed and supported by the Irish Association of Social Work (www.IASW.ie/about-social-work).

1   *Recognising the inherent dignity of every human being in our actions, our words and our intent.* Social workers are asked to ensure that those who have been harmed and those who have been accused or

found to have harmed a child are treated with dignity, respect and transparency. Irrespective of how a person may have acted, social workers are asked to hold on to the belief and the hope that a person can act differently if presented with a different set of circumstances or indeed given the opportunity to do so. Every person has value and strengths that should be recognised, promoted and enhanced for the benefit of safeguarding children.

2   *Promoting human rights and, perhaps more commonly, balancing the competing rights of individuals.* In child protection and welfare, this is particularly apt as, in the majority of our work, we are balancing the parent's right to autonomy and life choices, allowing them to show that they can provide safe care for a child, while also recognising the child's ongoing need and right for safety and protection and their family life.

3   *Promoting social justice.* This typically relates to challenging discrimination, respecting diversity, addressing inequality in terms of income and opportunity, challenging unjust policy or practice, and building social networks. Social workers are asked to ensure that our practice is non-discriminatory or anti-oppressive, and that we are promoting the use of naturally occurring social networks and actively supporting, informing and challenging social policy in areas that impact on our service-users.

4   *Promoting the right to self-determination.* We do this by ensuring that people have the right to make their own choices and decisions, provided that this does not affect the rights and freedoms of others. In child protection and welfare, this means that we are challenged to ensure that children and their families are supported to address harm or future harm to their child through means and actions that they determine, as long as these actions promote the child's safety and wellbeing. All persons should be allowed to consider and show that their own solutions can achieve safety for their child before the State is asked to impose its solutions.

5   *Promoting the right to participation.* This is achieved by ensuring that we build on the self-esteem and capabilities of people, promoting their full involvement and participation in all decisions and actions that affect their lives. This means ensuring that children, parents and relevant others have an active role in planning and decision-making, and that our practice supports co-produced assessments and plans that speak to how a child will be kept safe.

6   *Professional integrity through applying our code of ethics and by organisations creating conditions in the workplace where their own codes are discussed, evaluated and upheld.* Social workers need to operate within an environment that supports and promotes our values in practice, and the organisation must align itself to ensure that we can practise in line with our code of values and ethics.

Values underpinning our child protection and welfare systems

Like most other professions, social work does not exist within a vacuum. Practice typically operates within a much wider system of influence that includes factors such as human rights conventions, legislation, government policy, organisational policy, and regulatory standards. It is also influenced by political ideologies, findings from child-abuse inquiries and evolving practice learning. Many authors, including Gilbert (1997) and Parton (2014), have written extensively on the myriad political, social and organisational factors and their impact on social work. This combination of influences is what I refer to as the child protection and welfare system. These systems are complex and multi-faceted, and when examined are interestingly and typically underpinned by their own values or belief system. In exploring these systems and their value base, I reference the work completed by Gilbert et al. (2011) and Parton (2014) where they examined and identified the different types of systems orientations that exist. These orientations are classified as child protection, family service, child rights and an emerging public health approach. Gilbert et al. categorise these orientations across a number of key underpinning perspectives, and Parton further explores aspects of the public-health-oriented system.

Table 1: Poverty Measures by Age Group, 2019

	Child Protection	**Family Service**	**Child Focus**
Driver for intervention	Parents being neglectful and abusive towards children (maltreatment)	The family unit needs assistance	The individual child's needs in a present and future perspective: societies need healthy and contributory citizens

	Child Protection	**Family Service**	**Child Focus**
Role of the State	Sanctioning: the State functions as 'watchdog' to ensure safety	Parental support: the State seeks to strengthen family relations	Paternalistic/ defamilialisation: the State assumes parental role but seeks to refamilialise child by foster home/ kinship/ adoption
Problem frame	Individual/ moralistic	Social/ psychological (system, poverty, racism, etc.)	Child development and unequal outcomes for children
Mode of intervention	Legalistic/ investigative	Therapeutic/needs assessment	Early intervention and regulatory/ needs assessment
Aim of intervention	Protection/harm reduction	Prevention/social bonding	Promote wellbeing via social investment and/or equal opportunity
State–parent relationship	Adversarial	Partnership	Substitutive/ partnership
Balance of rights	Children's/parent's rights enforced by legal means	Parents' rights to family life mediated by professional social workers	Children's rights/parental responsibility

Source: 'The Politics of Child Protection: An Introduction', Chapter 1 from The Politics of Child Protection *(Parton, 2014)*

While no jurisdiction would be oriented solely into one system, many would have greater or lesser leanings towards an orientation, depending on legislation, policy and political ideologies, etc. Looking at Gilbert and Parton's work, we see the inherent or underpinning value base within each system:

1   Child-protection oriented systems tend to see parents as dangerous people who are wilfully harmful to their children. They are not to be trusted, and the State should intervene strongly if they do not co-operate fully with the State's expectations. In this context, social

workers should adopt a blaming attitude, and parents should be forced to take up services in order to 'fix them'. If parents do not agree, then we should forcibly remove their children, the belief being that they don't, or indeed won't, have the insight or capacity to understand their children's needs and, therefore, will never be able to protect them from danger.

2   Family-support oriented systems tend to believe parents to be vulnerable, needing help and support to deal with problems that have affected their ability to care for their children. In this context, social workers should approach families with a sense of compassion and understanding, and create a sense of hope that they can learn to keep their children safe with the support of others. There is a belief that the vast majority of families can be helped, and intervention should strengthen and empower, not blame and punish. Every effort should be made to understand, to involve and to adopt a strengths-and-solution focus to our work.

3   Child rights systems are oriented around the idea that children have a right to safety irrespective of their parents' issues and their capacity to achieve 'good enough' parenting. Social workers are asked to intervene to help parents, but support should be focused on improving the child's circumstances as meaningfully and quickly as possible. If we deem the parenting approach to be 'not good enough', it is better that the children's needs be met somewhere else, and the State should provide a substitute parent.

4   Public-health oriented systems tend to widen their focus from individual level and see child abuse as a symptom of much bigger societal issues. Parents are victims of the inequalities of society that have created the circumstances in which children are more likely to get harmed. In addition, Parton (2014) also highlights that:

> Child abuse can therefore be manifested at the institutional or societal levels, as well as within families and with individuals. The activities of certain institutions, such as schools and the church, the processes of racial discrimination, social class exploitation, gender violence and the role of government .... are all potentially implicated.

5   Social work intervention here should be in the social justice realm, advocating for such inequalities and injustices to be addressed, leading to far fewer vulnerabilities within family systems and, indeed, preventing the exploitation of those more likely to experience abuse and neglect. While severe abuse can be found across society and in all family types, welfare concerns and neglect are undoubtedly found in families who are disproportionally affected by inequalities in society, as evidenced by many authors, including Featherstone et al. (2019) and Bywaters et al. (2020).

The Irish child protection system orientation and the impact on social work

Many authors have already documented rich and informed history of the development of the child protection and welfare system in Ireland, including most recently Buckley and Nolan (2013), Buckley and Burns (2015), Whelan (2018) and Burns and McGregor (2019). Certainly Buckley and Burns (2015), and more recently Whelan (2018), have indicated a number of factors suggesting that the Irish system is still firmly rooted in a more child-protection oriented system, with attempts to move towards a more family-centred and child-rights perspective. Whelan, having examined the evolving nature of Ireland's systems, concludes:

> The system principle upon which it is based, is broadly similar to Gilbert's (2012) summary of a modern day 'child protection' approach where the identification and investigation of abuse remains centrally important largely due to high profile child abuse inquires and scandals…. However, then and now, concern continues to be expressed about the over emphasis on child abuse investigation within the system, the focus on blaming parents and the high level of attrition as children and families move between each stage of the child protection process. (Whelan 2018)

I would like to focus on three key areas which I feel have greatest recent resonance to evidence further how the Irish system remains strongly oriented to the child-protection perspective, and how this prevailing orientation is impacting on social work and ethical relationship-based practice.

Legislative and policy context

Since the enactment of the Child Care Act in 1991, there has been little in the way of evolving and progressive legislation to give further meaningful legal grounding to the insertion of children's rights under Article 42A of the Constitution in 2015, or to give renewed expression to the type of child-protection system that this core legislation defined. Whilst the Act sought a more family service and child-rights orientation, the balance continues to lean toward child protection as evidenced by:

1   The adversarial nature of applications and the need to meet thresholds of proof akin to criminal law have increasingly placed social workers in the role of investigating and evidencing parental failure, to the extent that relationship-based practice has been significantly undermined, as cited by Halton et al. (2018).

2   High expectations and standards of social work practice are undermined by the absence of a statutory framework to support greater interagency collaboration in the delivery of integrated child-protection and welfare responses. Holding statutory responsibility without the necessary authority to affect this responsibility typically leaves social work practitioners/managers held to account for ensuring a level of co-ordination that is not within their full power or authority.

3   Increased awareness of the obligation to promote the welfare of children and safeguard them from potential harm has resulted in a welcome growth in referrals of adults disclosing childhood abuse. However, in the absence of robust legislative clarity or authority, developing case law has determined that the safeguarding function requires social workers to step into the role of forensic investigators. Worryingly, relationship-based practice has been significantly undermined by the weight of fair-procedure policies to address what is, in essence, an absence of law and explicit authority.

Political context

Parton argued:

> Social work has always attempted to mediate between a number of potentially contradictory complex demands – care and control, empowerment and regulation, and promoting and safeguarding individual children's welfare. (Parton, 2014)

Looking through a political lens, there is often both an implicit and an explicit expectation that social work should seek to balance and mediate between these perspectives and the tension that exists therein, with the expectation that a perfect equilibrium can be achieved at all times, i.e. intervene effectively to ensure a child is safe, ensure that everyone is fully engaged and co-operating with the intervention, and support the family to the highest degree to prevent the child's removal.

If a social worker balances in favour of supporting the family, they can be accused of not focusing sufficiently on the child's safety. If they strongly promote the child's rights, it can be said that they are potentially undermining parental rights. If they encourage co-operation and sharing of information, it can be said that they are not respecting a family's privacy. Mediating these perspectives requires social workers to make decisions where we must continually offset or compare the value of one outcome against the value of another, accepting that there is uncertainty in both choices.

Every decision in a child-protection context will have both positive and negative outcomes for a child and their family. A child may be protected from further harm, but this may also involve being separated from siblings or adults they love and who love them. Therefore, it must be understood and accepted that if society wants social workers to offer a compassionate but balanced, safety-focused, evidence-informed, rights-based and collaborative approach to how we intervene, then our practice has to be based on the ability to form good working relationships in the most challenging of circumstances. This is where our ethics become critically important as we are asked to sustain meaningful collaborative working relationships in situations where we are also required to make complex and difficult judgements that are inevitably distressing and highly emotive.

Understandably, society and the general population are rarely exposed to social work practice, and thus are unlikely to understand the true complexity of our task. In reality, most social workers feel that they are walking on a very high tightrope, with no safety net to catch their almost inevitable fall from high expectations of always arriving at the perfect decision, while balancing all the varying perspectives and outcomes.

Political systems tend, particularly when things go wrong, to move swiftly to judge and to demand minimum or no error, moving away from a balanced perspective to creating an expectation that social work decision-making should always be perfect. The expectation of expertise and excellence in practice is accepted, but the concept of perfect practice is a completely different matter. We would never expect a child not to become unwell because we have a health system, nor crime not to occur to a child because we have a justice system, and yet somehow there is often both an explicit and an implicit expectation that no child should be harmed because we have a child-protection and welfare service, or indeed a solely responsible child-protection and welfare agency with singularly responsible professionals.

Organisational context

Inevitably within this expectation, a social worker's practice and their ability to live to their values will be affected. If the system understands the complexity of the task, yet demands perfection in achieving it, social workers will undoubtedly falter and, in doing so, most likely compromise their values. Fear and anxiety about not achieving perfection are then managed by having less of a focus on intervening in a value-based way with the hope of making a difference to the child and family, i.e. seeking to do the 'right thing'. Avoidance of any perceived criticism or failure is thus achieved by doing 'things right', i.e. following defined regulated procedures and processes, and completing such processes and forms within required timeframes and other associated performance measures. As Munro has stated:

> Helping children is a human process. When the bureaucratic aspects of the work become too dominant, the heart of the work is lost. (Munro 2011b)

In essence, the values of social work practice are lost, and the relationship-based work that is central to social work is diminished in favour of organisational procedures created to manage the impossible expectation of getting it right. As Buckley stated:

> [T]here is a danger that over-concentration on simplistic organisational-centred auditing processes and performance measures will stifle the continued development of child protection work. This places a high priority on tangible outputs and ignores the crucial elements of relationship and principle based work. (Buckley 2008)

Therefore, the conflict emerges, that the practitioner is continuously faced with the dilemma of operating in line with the systems expectations and the organisation procedures. Regulatory standards and system demands for performance against such standards take precedence over operating to our expected code of ethics and the less measurable relationship-based practice. Inevitably, the system will prevail, and the practitioner will find an increased inability to work to their values and to the core beliefs that brought them into the work, their job satisfaction will diminish, and they will either become apathetic to this work or they will simply leave the employment.

Building an effective CPW system that promotes our values and supports the balancing act

It would clearly appear from a legislative and policy context that Ireland wants a child-protection system where social workers intervene in private family life in a necessary, consistent but proportionate way. We all want children to be safe from harm, but we also do not want family life unnecessarily disrupted or rash decisions made about a child that would see children removed unnecessarily and cause huge pain to a family. The system should be able to support families to overcome difficulties, and to maintain the integrity of the family because that is where children do best and that is what the law and society asks us to do. The following key changes would support building consistent ethical practice and creating a sustainable system.

Legislative and policy reform

At present, the Department of Children, Equality, Disability, Integration and Youth (DCEDIY) is undertaking a review of the Child Care Act, 1991. Based on the collective view of key stakeholders, documented in *A Report on the Finding of an Open Policy Debate on the Review of the Child Care Act 1991* (DCEDIY 2017) and the *Review of the Child Care Act 1991* July 2020 Consultation Paper (DCEDIY 2020), some key and relevant recommendations are emerging which would support shifting us away from a child-protection oriented system. These would include:

- *A shift to a stronger children's rights and family-service orientation* – In addition to the child's right to safety and having their best interests and participation at the centre of decision-making, this should also include a right to family in the broader context of the definition of the child's family and friend network. These existing supports can act both as advocates for the parent or child, can be members of a safety network supporting a child-protection safety plan, or can provide temporary longer-term family-based alternative care.

- *Necessary and proportionate authority* – If Tusla is being asked by the State under the Act to hold any statutory responsibility, then due consideration must be given to the explicit statutory authority it holds in this regard. All authority should be proportionate but explicit, and centred on placing the social worker as safeguarding and protecting the child's rights, providing the social worker with the ability to be the facilitator of many essential processes, including information sharing, co-ordination/integration of professional services, social network finding and their inclusion in decision-making.

- *An inquiry approach to proceedings and not a criminal trial* – Undoubtedly social workers will need to provide evidence of the harm and long-term impact of harm to a child to support a Court in making a determination regarding the welfare of the child. However, establishing such process of adjudication on the need to evidentially prove parental failure, while simultaneously requiring a social worker to sustain relationship-based working presents a significant conflict. Detailed analysis by Halton et al. (2018) cites the need for a 'less formal and more inquisitorial system of child welfare' as a key means to address the adversarial nature. Promotion of a greater range of legally endorsed collaborative and mediated approaches to decision-making that still promote child and parental rights would certainly sustain better ethical practice. All efforts should seek to avoid social workers being perceived as the sole adversary of essential parental rights.

- *Interagency Co-operation* – A key theme in all the reports arising from the consultation on the review of the Act is the need for greater interagency co-operation and the statutory basis to support such participation. While the Act originally placed an obligation on the then Health Boards to promote the welfare of children, the subsequent shift of this responsibility to the much narrower remit of the Child and Family Agency has seen a lack of clarity on the responsibility of other sectors not only to report concerns but to play an active part in the promotion and protection of children. Social workers need to work in a system where there is a duty to work together, not just a commitment.

Political and regulatory reform – promoting accountability

Practice should always be open to scrutiny, and social work decision-making should be accountable to the public and those public representatives that we serve. However, to be accountable means to take responsibility for results, good or bad, and in child-protection and welfare work it means applying lessons learned in order to improve future results. Blame, on the other hand, is more focused on the past and on punishing the person who made the error. There is also a risk that the demand for accountability in poor decision-making in child-protection practice becomes separated from the wider systemic issues that see some children more likely referred to statutory child-protection services. As Parton highlighted in reference to the UK system, there is a risk in an Irish context that pushing responsibility for child protection onto one agency, and then primarily onto one profession, might equally promote a climate where:

> Political outrage and concern has been so focused on the problems and 'failures' of the child protection system that there has been a failure to seriously address the problem of child maltreatment. (Parton 2014)

The review of the Child Care Act may provide an opportunity for necessary and open debate on the system orientation that the Act and, indeed, the political system wish to endorse. This would, in turn, assist in providing a better understanding of expected practice, a more proactive engagement in understanding good practice, and not just reactive responses to perceived failures when they occur. Greater engagement with and from the political system would, in turn, promote a learning culture within child-protection organisations that centres accountability in continuous improvement and seeks to educate the wider system on what works in achieving effective safety and wellbeing for children. Indeed, there needs to be a recognition that not all harm can be prevented, and that the organisation and the wider system are continuously learning how to be more effective and to minimise errors. The role and review of regulatory standards being currently undertaken by the Health Information and Quality Authority (HIQA) also promise to support greater accountability without quality measures being highly reliant on compliance with standard process. The assessment of quality against such standards also needs to broaden to include the assessment of effectiveness of all partners in the child-protection and welfare system as a whole.

Organisational reform – interagency and intra-agency considerations

A greater mandate and remit for social workers and Tusla to co-ordinate cross-agency responses to child-protection and welfare concerns are essential and, as mentioned earlier, need to be supported with legislative authority and set within a supportive policy framework. If statutory authority is mandated only in guidance and negotiated protocols, then there is a strong argument to revisit the remit of the Child and Family Agency to ensure that early help and responses to harm are more co-ordinated and robust. Certainly, the Task Force set up in 2012 to support the establishment of the Agency states in the preface of its final report:

> [T]he fragmentation and silos that exist in services is the systemic cause of the failure to meet children's needs. They [various reports] have repeatedly pointed to a lack of accountability amongst agencies and professionals and failure to meet the needs of the child with devastating result.

The report concluded that, in considering the kind of Agency that needed to be established, it was 'crucial that certain services for children are realigned from across a number of agencies into a single, comprehensive, integrated and accountable agency for children and families'. The Task Force also stated that if the vision for the Agency were not to be realised, social workers alone would be left to meet the needs of children, without integrated support of the necessary range of professional disciplines, and the State would continue to fail in its obligation to children. In reality, many of the service areas due to form part of the integrated response were not included in the formation of the Agency, i.e. Public Health Nursing, Child and Adolescent Mental Health Services, youth-related services and psychology services. This, in turn, has resulted in a child-protection and welfare response that is primarily social-work led and leaves social workers and Agency with the challenge of securing interagency co-operation with very little mandate other than what can be tenuously agreed through commitments and cross-agency protocols.

Practice reform

As the IASW sets out:

> Social work aims to empower individuals, groups and communities to take charge of their own lives within their own environment and social context. It does this through its unique base which has developed from the integration of sociological, psychological and other relevant theories and practice.

Therefore, all effective child-protection and welfare social work practice must also operate in an environment where knowledge, skills and values are promoted, encouraged and actively supported. If I define 'practice' as the actual application of an idea or method, as opposed to the theory relating to it, then I am referring to both the theoretical and evidence-informed knowledge held by a social worker and the skills required to implement that knowledge into day-to-day decision-making and interventions in a child and family's life. I am also most importantly referring to the values or ethical code that informs how I apply my knowledge and skills and how I work with the child and family to achieve the best outcome. Thus, achieving effective, consistent child-protection work requires a consistent practice approach that is embedded with these values, promotes and encourages the use of effective skills and allows for existing or new knowledge to be incorporated into that approach. It is a combination of both process (the 'how' we intervene that achieves best results) and content (what is informing our intervention based on what we know is more effective). Turnell and Murphy (2017) refer to the use of a practice approach as:

> …a vehicle to drill down into its practice to create a learning organisation focused on how it is implementing its work, how it is reviewing its outcomes, success and failures, and allowing it to continuously adapt and change as necessary keeping to the key principles of the approach.

As referred to earlier, the drive for consistency and quality of decision-making is sometimes believed to exist solely within the realm of standard processes, i.e. if we all follow the same process and complete the same forms, then we will achieve the same outcomes. However, making good decisions about child protection and welfare is not like a manufacturing production line or a formulaic chemical equation. It might improve how quickly a decision is made, it might ensure that everyone is following the same process and timelines, and it might encourage practitioners to capture information consistently against some standard assessment criteria. I am less confident, though, that standard processes alone improve the consistency and quality of decision-making or the quality of the social work engagement with the child and family.

Procedures can tell you what to do at a point in time, but they can rarely tell you how to do it in a way that makes sense to the child and family. They may encourage a focus on performance on prescribed timelines but, beyond the accepted expectation that we immediately respond to imminent and serious risk, the timeliness of further responses is relative to the circumstances of each case and the decisions that are required to achieve meaningful safety for that child in their family. Implementing new policy and procedures without an agreed approach will achieve limited effect, as the breadth of expectation continuously created and seen to be addressed through a wide range of procedures or processes will eventually become too wide to be effectively understood and implemented.

What must also be understood is that there is no existing perfect practice approach in child protection and welfare, as its emergence would have resulted in worldwide adoption as a means to resolving our approach to child abuse. Therefore, one has continuously to build towards a robust and workable approach using current developed practitioner wisdom, to ensure that it is inherently embedded with the principles and values of how we want to work with children and families, and to ensure that it can incorporate current and new knowledge of what we already know from research and evidence-based knowledge. Consistency in practice is best achieved not by obedience or compliance to procedure but by greater alignment to our values and consistency in the way in which we want to work with children and families, and the type of changes we need to see in the behaviour of those responsible for children that keeps them safe. Depth of practice will be achieved through continuous learning of what works best in a range of different types of scenarios, using and deepening our flexibility of the approach as a means of strengthening it, and then supporting it with evidence and guidance. The initial focus of our practice must always be the safety of a child. Once safety is assured overtime, then the child and family can, if willing and able, begin to address further the longer-term more complex individual problems that will, it is hoped, lead to an overall improvement in wellbeing for the family and the children.

Supporting a relationship-based practice approach

It must be understood that the practice approach is being applied not to replace other professional knowledge and thinking, but rather to enhance how we utilise and share our existing professional knowledge and thinking with others. The organisation will need to consider further alignment to the practice approach so that the relevant policies, procedures, guidance and forms, and the IT systems that support them, can effectively encourage practice breadth and depth, and ensure that practice analysis, plans and decisions are recorded and that meaningful information can be drawn from these records that allows us to examine how effective we are at achieving the outcomes we want. Relationship-based and reflective practice approaches are inherently more time-demanding, and therefore the system inevitably has to consider how it can support giving practitioners more time to achieve depth and quality. Managing demand has to be considered against performance expectations and consideration of better performance measures that promote more effective practice and practice outcomes.

Walsh (2008) states that moving to reflective practice in child-protection and welfare work is 'not without frustration, struggle and disappointment'. She also cites many authors' work in defining reflective practice, focusing it on a created 'safe space' to talk about the impact of the work, while also creating an environment where reflecting on this impact allows us to learn how not to minimise the negative impact it could have on ourselves and our relationships in practice. Utilising a practice approach that consistently incorporates practice tools with learning and reflective methods (e.g. supervision, group supervision, reflective practice workshops) strengthens and endorses such reflection to be a core aspect of the practice and not something that is dependent on the preference of the worker or the quality of the supervisor. Practice only deepens when we actually practise, and then spend time reflecting on what worked, what didn't and how we might improve. Creating a learning organisation that is also accountable requires the opening-up of practice and making it visible – visible in terms of the direct work we do and visible in terms of the impact and outcomes we are having.

Unfortunately, one of the most pervasive challenges in child-protection and welfare work is that it is invisible work until something goes wrong. Equally, much of the data produced tell us very little about the lived experiences of children or parents, nor are they the type of outcome-oriented data that would show how interventions are effective. It is incumbent on social workers to show the complexity of their task, the complexity of the work, and their skill of being able to forge relationships in the most challenging of circumstances, as well as their skill in navigating safety for children. This has to be balanced against the privacy and confidentiality of the people in the work, and we have to overcome the fear and anxiety that is associated with showing our practice. Opening up practice in this complex emotional work also opens practitioners to the fear of criticism and blame. Therefore, leaders of practice must stay alongside it, in order to understand and support how it is utilised, must stay behind it in order to support the wider changes that are essential to encourage it and, most importantly, must stand in front of it when it is challenged.

Conclusion

Social work had its foundation in relationship-based and ethically principled practice. In meeting our professional obligations, social workers in child-protection work are held to an appropriately high standard in the performance of our professional duties. It is compliance to our professional code of conduct and ethics that continues to be this standard. Creating effective safety for children in an emotionally laden environment where co-operation is sometimes limited, where interventions are typically fraught, and expectations are inevitably high will never be easy. Social workers rely on our practice and our shared values to sustain working relationships, to empower change and improve the lives of children and families. However, this requires an environment and system that support this practice, and it requires social workers to ensure that our approach to practice is consistently embedded with those principles. This requires organisations, advocacy groups and regulators to lead for change to the current system that can better support this practice. The profession must also continue to commit to these principles within our work, and also to influence social policy that shapes the child-protection and welfare system. If the profession is not central in leading for this change, others will – or perhaps they won't – put social work practice and social work values at the heart of it.

References

Biestek, F. (1957), *The Casework Relationship*, Chicago: Loyola University Press.

Buckley, H. (2002), *Child Protection and Welfare: Innovations and Interventions*, Dublin: IPA.

Buckley, H. (2008), 'Heading for Collision? Managerialism, Social Science and the Irish Child Protection System' in Burns, K., and Lynch, D. (eds), *Child Protection and Welfare Social Work: Contemporary Themes and Practice Perspectives*, Dublin: A&A Farmar

Buckley, H., and Burns, K. (2015), 'Child Welfare and Protection in Ireland: Déjà Vu All Over Again' in Christie, A., Featherstone, B., Quin, S. and Walsh, T. (eds), *Social Work in Ireland: Changes and Continuities*, London: Palgrave Macmillan, pp 51–70.

Buckley, H., and O'Nolan, C. (2013), *An Examination of Recommendations from Inquiries into Events in Families and their Interactions with State Services, and their Impact on Policy and Practice*, Dublin: DCYA, Government Publications.

Burns, K., and McGregor, C. (2019), 'Child Protection and Welfare Systems in Ireland: Continuities and Discontinuities of the Present' in: Merkel-Holguin, L., Fluke, J., and Krugman R. (eds), *National Systems of Child Protection: Child Maltreatment* (Contemporary Issues in Research and Policy), vol. 8. Springer, Cham. Available at https://doi.org/10.1007/978-3-319-93348-1_7

Burns, K., Christie, A., and O'Sullivan, S. (2020), 'Findings from a Longitudinal Qualitative Study of Child Protection Social Workers' Retention: Job Embeddedness, Professional Confidence and Staying Narratives', *British Journal of Social Work*, vol. 50, issue 5, July, pp 1363–81. Available at https://doi.org/10.1093/bjsw/bcz083

Bywaters, P. et al. (2020), *The Child Welfare Inequalities Project: Final Report*, The Nuffield Foundation with the University of Huddersfield. Available at https://mk0nuffieldfounpg9ee.kinstacdn.com/wp-content/uploads/2019/11/CWIP-Overview-Final-V4.pdf

Child Care Act, 1991. Available at http://www.irishstatutebook.ie/eli/1991/act/17/enacted/en/html

Constitution of Ireland, The (1937), Dublin: Government Publications.

CORU (2019), *Social Work Registration Board Code of Professional Conduct and Ethics*, Social Worker Registration Board. Available at https://www.coru.ie/files-codes-of-conduct/swrb-code-of-professional-conduct-and-ethics-for-social-workers.pdf

Department of Children, Equality, Disability, Integration and Youth (DCEDIY) (2020), *Review of the Child Care Act 1991, July 2020 Consultation Paper*, Dublin: Government Publications. Available at https://www.gov.ie/en/publication/14c93-review-of-the-child-care-act-1991-july-2020-consultation-paper/

Department of Children and Youth Affairs (DCYA) (2012), *Report of the Task Force on the Child and Family Support Agency*, Dublin: Government Publications.

Department of Children and Youth Affairs (DCYA) (2017), *Report on the Findings of an Open Policy Debate on the Review of the Child Care Act 1991*, Dublin: Government Publications. Available at https://www.gov.ie/pdf/?file=https://assets.gov.ie/27771/64c5d904b9ba4deab2ec9683c9d2fad7.pdf#page=1

Duggan, C., and Corrigan, C. (2009), *A Literature Review of Interagency Work with a Particular Focus on Children Services*, CAAB Research Report No. 4, Dublin: CAAB. Available at https://assets.gov.ie/39972/58446fb5692146e0a7516b3d4af5e701.pdf

Featherstone, B. et al. (2019), 'Poverty, Inequality, Child Abuse and Neglect: Changing the Conversation Across the UK in Child Protection?', *Children and Youth Services Review*, vol. 97, February, pp 127–33. Available at https://doi.org/10.1016/j.childyouth.2017.06.009

Gilbert, N. (1997), *Combatting Child Abuse: International Perspectives and Trends*, New York: Oxford University Press.

Gilbert, N., Parton, N., and Skivenes, M. (2011), *Child Protection Systems: International Trends and Orientations*, New York: Oxford University Press.

Halton, C., Harold, G., Murphy, A., and Walsh, E. (2018), *A Social and Economic Analysis of the Use of Legal Services (SEALS) in the Child and Family Agency (Tusla)*, Cork: University College Cork.

Ingram, R., and Smith, M. (2018), 'Relationship-based Practice: Emergent Themes in Social Work Literature', Insight 41, Iriss. Available at https://www.iriss.org.uk/resources/insights/relationship-based-practice-emergent-themes-social-work-literature

International Federation of Social Workers (IFSW) (2014), quoted on Irish Association of Social Workers (IASW) website. Available at https://www.iasw.ie/about-social-work

International Federation of Social Workers (IFSW) (2018), *Global Social Work Statement of Ethical Principles*, IFSW. Available at https://www.ifsw.org/global-social-work-statement-of-ethical-principles/

Irish Association of Social Workers (IASW), 'About Social Work'. Available at https://www.iasw.ie/about-social-work

Mintz, S. (2019), *Beyond Happiness and Meaning: Transforming your Life Through Ethical Behaviour*, USA: Gatekeeper Press.

Munro, E. (2008), *Effective Child Protection* (2nd edn), London: Sage.

Munro, E. (2011), *The Munro Review of Child Protection: Final Report. A Child Centred System*, London: Department for Education.

Parton, N. (2014), *The Politics of Child Protection: Contemporary Developments and Future Directions*, London: Palgrave Macmillan.

Redmond, B. et al. (2010), *The Retention of Social Workers in the Health Services: An Evidence-Based Assessment Project Report*, Dublin: University College Dublin.

Skehill, C. (1999), *The Nature of Social Work in Ireland*, Lampeter, Wales: The Edwin Mellen Press.

Turnell, A., and Murphy, T. (2017), *Signs of Safety Comprehensive Briefing Paper* (4th edn), Perth: Resolutions.

Walsh, C. (2008), 'The Critical Role of Reflection and Process in Child Protection and Welfare Work' in Burns, K., and Lynch, D. (eds), *Child Protection and Welfare Social Work: Contemporary Themes and Practice Perspectives*, Dublin: A&A Farmar.

Whelan, S. (2018), *At the Front Door: Child Protection Reporting in a Changing Policy and Legislative Context*, thesis for the degree of Doctor of Philosophy, Trinity College Dublin.

CHAPTER 5

THE ROLE OF PUBLIC POLICY IN THE REFORM OF YOUTH DETENTION IN IRELAND: PROGRESS AND LEARNING

Ursula Kilkelly[1]

Introduction

In 1992, Ireland ratified the United Nations Convention on the Rights of the Child, committing to protect the rights of children in all areas of their lives. Given Ireland's historically poor treatment of children, there was much to do to meet the Convention's minimum standards. Nearly three decades after ratification, Ireland's children's rights record is much improved, and it leads internationally in having a dedicated Minister for Children, a national children's policy framework, a longitudinal study of children's lives and outcomes, a Constitution with express protection for children's rights, and an independent office of Ombudsman for Children with responsibility to protect and promote children's rights. All of these measures reflect the status children's issues now receive in government, and although there is much still to do, important foundations are in place on which greater progress can be built.

---

1   The author would like to thank her Research Assistant, Laura Lanigan, for her help in contributing to this chapter.

Significant progress has also been made in the treatment of especially vulnerable children, including children who come into conflict with the law. Under the Convention, children in conflict with the law are entitled to treatment consistent with their dignity and worth, taking account of their age and the desirability of their reintegration into society (Article 40). Detention must be a measure of last resort, and children deprived of liberty must be separated from adults and treated with dignity and respect and in a manner which takes account of the needs of persons of their age. When Ireland ratified the Convention, it lagged behind internationally in having no specialist youth justice system, limited formal means to divert children from court, and relatively high numbers of children in detention, including in adult prison where there was little chance of their needs being met. In the intervening years, reforms have taken place at every level, but especially in addressing the needs of some of the most vulnerable children, those who end up in detention. This chapter aims to examine the leading role that public policy has played in bringing about this reform. While examining the progress made to date, the piece reflects on the areas where challenges still remain.

Legislative reform

The Children Act, 2001

Despite many reviews and inquiries throughout the twentieth century, it was a parliamentary committee report in 1992 that finally prompted an overhaul of Ireland's youth justice system, which had until that time been governed by the Children Act, 1908. The Report of the Dáil Select Committee on Crime: Juvenile Crime, its Causes and its Remedies (1992) made a series of enlightened recommendations, including increasing the age of criminal responsibility to 12 years, introducing specialised youth justice agencies, placing diversion on a statutory basis, and abolishing the imprisonment of children. The report reflected a commitment to fulfilling the standards in the Convention on the Rights of the Child and other UN rules and recommendations. According to the Committee, it was 'self-evident' that our claim to

> a valued place in the community of civilised nations depends heavily on our performance in this particularly sensitive area of civil liberties and public policy. Our provision must match

the standards laid down by these documents. (Dáil Select Committee 1992)

When finally enacted, the Children Act, 2001 reflected these standards, and it drew on international best practice, specifically the lessons of the New Zealand model with its heavy reliance on family conferencing and restorative justice (Kilkelly 2006). The Act was innovative in setting out key children's rights principles in the treatment of children by the courts, and it drew on New Zealand law, including provisions designed to keep troubled children with welfare needs out of the criminal justice system. Crucial among the provisions of the 2001 Act were: the definition of the child as a person under 18 years, which placed all children in conflict with the law under the remit of the youth justice system; the placement of the Garda Diversion Programme on a statutory basis; and the introduction of the family conference, which could be convened by the Probation Service on the order of the Children Court, as an alternative to conviction. The Act set out a range of community-based sanctions, designed to give effect to the principle in section 96 that detention must be a measure of last resort. It prohibited the imprisonment of children, and thereby set in train a series of legislative and policy measures that would ultimately lead to the establishment of a specialist detention facility for all children under 18 years referred by the courts. This is discussed further below.

The Youth Justice Review

Although the Children Act, 2001 was warmly welcomed as a modern framework for the treatment of children in conflict with the law, its implementation was piecemeal and frustrated by responsibility being fragmented across government departments. The *Youth Justice Review*, commissioned by the Department of Justice, Equality and Law Reform in 2005, was a timely analysis of the progress made in the implementation of the 2001 Act. Led by Sylda Langford, the Review consulted stakeholders and reviewed international trends in youth justice to support a number of far-reaching and pragmatic recommendations, including the legal and structural changes required to enhance the delivery of youth justice services in Ireland. The Review's most important finding was that the Children Act, 2001 provides 'a sound legal basis for a modern youth justice system and what is now required is for it to be fully implemented and supported by the necessary resources for that implementation (Department of Justice,

Equality and Law Reform 2006, p. 7). Additional conclusions concerned the need to emphasise prevention and early intervention, co-ordinate and integrate services, promote existing interagency co-operation and ensure that detention was a last resort through the resourcing of community-based sanctions.

The progressive thrust of the Report stood in stark contrast to the 'punitive turn' that was underway in other western jurisdictions at that time (Muncie 2008), and it was remarkable for drawing instead on child-centred approaches in New Zealand and Canada that highlighted the importance of diversion, specialisation and a whole government approach to youth justice (Department of Justice, Equality and Law Reform 2006, pp 25–6). The Report's most significant recommendation was the establishment of a unified Youth Justice Service, under the aegis of the Department of Justice, which, the Report proposed, would have the remit to develop youth justice policy with linkages to other areas of national child-related strategy. In a move that was to clarify further the scope of the youth justice system, the Review recommended that the Youth Justice Service take responsibility for detention of offending children under 18 years of age. Thus, it recommended moving responsibility for the children detention schools from the Department of Education to the Youth Justice Service, and bringing 16- and 17-year-olds from the prison estate into the education-focused model, which should become 'the objective for all children under 18 years in detention' (Department of Justice, Equality and Law Reform 2006, p. 9). As pragmatic as they were far reaching, the *Review*'s recommendations, which were accepted by government and implemented without delay, were to have a very significant effect on the direction of youth justice in Ireland, as the next section now explains, bringing it into line with international children's rights standards.

New leadership in youth justice

At the time of the *Youth Justice Review*, government responsibility for children was also under consideration and, in 2005, the National Children's Office became the Office of the Minister for Children, accompanied by a 'super-junior' ministry with dedicated funding and shared responsibility for children's policy and services across key government departments (Kilkelly 2008, p. 17). In 2008, this expanded to become the Office of the Minister for Children and Youth Affairs (OMCYA) with a remit to 'harmonise policy issues that affect children in areas including youth justice, children and young people's participation and cross-cutting initiatives for children' (Office of the Minister for Children and Youth Affairs 2009, p. 3). In 2007, then, although the new Irish Youth Justice Service was established as an agency of the Department of Justice, in a creative move, its staff were drawn from different government departments and, in reality, it was bi-located between Justice and OMCYA.

When a full government Department of Children and Youth Affairs (DCYA) was established following the publication in 2010 of the Report of the Commission to Enquire into Child Abuse ('The Ryan Report'), the decision effectively to keep the Irish Youth Justice Service in the new Department of Children and Youth Affairs reflected an important commitment to ensure that youth justice remained connected to the wider areas of children's policy, in line with the recommendation of the *Youth Justice Review*. This approach was consolidated when DCYA adopted the new national policy framework – *Better Outcomes, Brighter Futures* – in 2014, incorporating the *Youth Justice Action Plan 2014–2018*, which is set out below. A recent review of the implementation of the Action Plan confirmed the importance to the implementation of youth justice that it shared its administrative home with other areas of children's policy and services (Kilkelly and Forde 2019), in the Department of Children and Youth Affairs, in a way that ensured that youth justice was informed by and connected to the leadership and policy that were active in other priority children's areas. In this regard, it is extremely disappointing that with the formation of the new Government following the General Election in 2020, responsibility for youth justice returned to the newly configured Department of Justice, with the consequent disbandment of the Youth Justice Service. It is, as yet, unclear whether a dedicated unit within the Department of Justice will be given responsibility for policy and leadership in this area, but either way, the crucial link with children's policy has been broken. Importantly, however, responsibility for child detention ('Oberstown') has remained with the Department of Children, Equality, Disability, Integration and Youth.

Youth justice policy

In 2008, in line with the recommendations of the *Youth Justice Review*, the new Youth Justice Service developed Ireland's first national strategy in the area – *Tackling Youth Crime* (Irish Youth Justice Service 2008). The Strategy committed to six high-level goals, including: providing leadership to the youth justice system; diverting young people from offending; promoting greater use of community sanctions; providing a safe and secure environment for detained children to assist their early reintegration into the community; and strengthening information and data sources to support more effective policies and services. Based on a child-centred approach, these high-level goals were accompanied by actions, with listed outcomes and performance indicators, ensuring that the Strategy was capable of measurement and review. This function was given to the National Youth Justice Oversight Group, appointed by the Minister, and consisting of representatives from government departments and criminal justice agencies, in an approach that was to begin to build relationships and partnerships that are key to the effective administration of youth justice to this day.

Tackling Youth Crime gave clear impetus to the implementation of the Children Act and for the first time identified strategic national priorities for youth justice. Apart from a number of important commitments relating to the operation of the youth justice system, it was significant that the Strategy included the implementation of 'a key element of the Government's youth justice reforms', namely 'the integration of our child-care policies and criminal justice policies' (Irish Youth Justice Service 2008, p. 17). As the first such national strategy, its focus was on 'getting key partners to engage, putting the right structures in place and delivering services more effectively' (Department of Justice and Equality 2013, p. 3). In a mid-term report on the implementation of the Strategy, the National Youth Justice Oversight Group found that the 'net effect of this combined effort has been to develop a more co-ordinated strategic approach, make better use of existing resources, create positive working relationships amongst stakeholders and deliver better outcomes for young people in trouble with the law and for the community in general' (Department of Justice and Equality 2013, p. 3).

The Strategy was followed in 2013 by the publication of the *National Youth Justice Action Plan 2014–2018*, which reflected a further embedding of youth justice within the national policy framework for children and its commitments to evidence-based policy-making and collaborative interagency working in the interests of young people. In terms of youth justice priorities, the *Action Plan* highlighted targeted interventions to reduce offending, promoting the use of community sanctions and providing a safe, secure environment for children deprived of liberty, designed to assist their reintegration into the community (Department of Justice and Equality 2013). It adopted a similar approach to the first Strategy, in identifying key deliverables and owners, and in this way, the *Action Plan* and the cross-departmental nature of the Irish Youth Justice Service (IYJS) helped to create a shared responsibility for the delivery of youth justice services and supports, in the interests of children, across the various agencies of the youth justice sector (Kilkelly and Forde 2019, p. 7). More generally, a review of the implementation of the *Action Plan* highlighted clear progress in the achievement of the goals set out, across all its high-level goals, identifying the leadership provided by IYJS and its connection to the broader area of children's policy as crucial elements in this success (Kilkelly and Forde 2019, p 34). Not all the goals were achieved, of course – the particular difficulties faced by children in care who 'cross over in the justice system' was one area singled out for mention in this respect (p. 35) – but the *Action Plan* served to consolidate the progressive direction of Irish youth justice, building on what had gone before.

In April 2021, government approval of the new youth justice strategy is awaited. Following a process of review and consultation which took place throughout 2020, this new strategy seeks to build on the approach of previous policies, giving continued impetus to the reform of youth justice in line with international children's rights obligations and best practice. From an administrative point of view, however, the transfer of responsibility for Garda diversion, bail and related youth justice services to the Department of Justice, together with the abolition of the Youth Justice Service, means that the implementation of the Strategy will fall under the leadership of that department. One important exception to this relates to responsibility for child detention, which remains with the new Department of Children, Equality, Disability, Integration and Youth. However progressive the content and direction of the Strategy, there is uncertainty, if not concern, about the future direction of youth justice, now that the connection with children's policy has begun to loosen. Only time will tell how significant this turns out to be.

Reform of child detention

Ireland has a long tradition of over-reliance on institutional care, with extensive use of residential facilities with frequently harsh and often abusive conditions (O'Sullivan and O'Donnell 2012). Many reviews inquired into the industrial and reformatory schools and the wider welfare system in the twentieth century, but it was not until 1985 that the Whitaker Report (the Commission of Enquiry into the Penal System) recommended the reform of child detention, proposing an enlightened model of detention for children, in small residential settings, with qualified and skilled staff (Sargent 2014). In 1983, the first purpose-built secure unit for children was established, separate to the prison system: Trinity House, which was designed to care for those considered 'unmanageable' in the 'special schools', was the responsibility of the Department of Education and, for the first time, it was to be staffed by care staff rather than prison officers.

Although the Children Act, 2001 clearly envisaged an end to child imprisonment, its fragmented approach to children above and below the age of 16 years made the achievement of associated reforms very difficult. In particular, the fact that under the Act, children under 16 years were detained in the children detention schools, falling under the responsibility of the Department of Education, and children over 16 years were detained in a children detention centre (principally St Patrick's Institution), under the responsibility of the Irish Prison Service/Department of Justice, effectively meant that the child-centred approach ended once a child turned 16. Although the (then) five children detention schools were not without their difficulties, the criticism levelled at St Patrick's Institution by national and international bodies was relentless and severe by comparison (Kilkelly 2006). Children detained in St Patrick's were subjected to a dehumanising prison regime that was completely at odds with their needs as children, and the continuation of the practice left Ireland out of line with our obligations under international law, including the Convention on the Rights of the Child. As noted above, the *Youth Justice Review* made several important recommendations with regard to the reform of child detention that finally brought into view an end to this practice. First, it recommended that the proposed Youth Justice Service take responsibility for all children under 18 years, ordered to be detained by the courts. This was a significant commitment to ensuring that all children under 18 years would enjoy their rights to education, care and reintegration under the Children Act, 2001, regardless of their age. To this end, the *Review* made two further recommendations – first, it recommended the transfer of policy and operational responsibility for the children detention schools from the Department of Education to the Youth Justice Service; and second, it recommended the transfer of responsibility for the detention of all children under 18 years from the Irish Prison Service to the Youth Justice Service (Department of Justice, Equality and Law Reform 2006, pp 44–5).

The *Youth Justice Review* was clear that all children in detention were to benefit from the education-focused model and, reflecting this priority, a capital investment of €26.6 million had been announced in 2000 by the Minister for Education and Science, allowing for refurbishment of the children detention schools on the Lusk campus (Kilkelly 2006, p. 199). To progress the recommendations of the *Youth Justice Review*, an Expert Group on Children Detention Schools was set up in April 2006 to initiate and oversee the planning needed to give effect to the extension of the children detention school model. This Group provided important leadership and structure to the complex process of both developing a new national approach to child detention, in line with best practice and international standards, and the various steps and stages necessary to transition towards a unified model of detention for all children under 18 years (Expert Group on Children Detention Schools 2006). From a legal point of view, a series of complex and interconnected measures was also required, including amendments of the 2001 Act by the Criminal Justice Act, 2006 and ultimately the Children Amendment Act, 2015, and associated statutory instruments, eventually to give responsibility for all children under 18 to Oberstown Children Detention Campus.

The *Youth Justice Strategy 2008–2010* had identified as a high-level goal to provide 'a safe and secure environment for detained children that will assist their early re-integration into the community' and to this end, IYJS committed to 'working in partnership with staff and management across the four children detention schools to develop the existing system and structures', in particular, working to ensure that 'the optimum staffing levels, financial resources, governance structures and policies and procedures' were in place to provide the best care and education of children and address their offending behaviour (Irish Youth Justice Service 2008, p. 17). The Strategy also made a commitment to collaboration with both the Vocational Education Committees and the Health Service Executive to ensure that detained children enjoyed access to the relevant education, health and social services to meet their needs (p. 18). The Strategy committed to implementing the report of the Expert Group on Children Detention Schools which, as noted above, provided important structure to the body of work associated with establishing a national children detention facility for all children up to 18 years (Expert Group on Children Detention Schools 2006).

By 2012, a government commitment of over €50 million had been secured to develop and expand the national detention facilities on the Lusk Campus. The *Youth Justice Action Plan 2014–2018* built on the previous commitment to ensure that the detention schools were based on a model of 'individualised care, education and rehabilitation to reduce the risk of re-offending and promote the positive re-integration of each young person into his or her family and community, where they will observe the law and are capable of making a positive and productive contribution to society' (Irish Youth Justice Service 2008, p. 24). As part of this development, the Strategy provided that a new 'national specialist team' would provide 'in-reach therapeutic services' for children in detention with 'social work, psychology, speech and language therapy, social care and addiction' services, aiming inter alia to reduce the need to remand children for the purpose of assessment. The Strategy reported that a 'forensic child and adolescent mental health service' was also planned (p. 24).

Many of these commitments gave effect to the Government's response to the Ryan Report, which had documented the appalling abuses that children had suffered in Irish institutions throughout the twentieth century. Acknowledging that the State had failed many children in its care, the *Ryan Report Implementation Plan* committed to a focus on improved outcomes for children, endorsing an approach whereby 'all policies, management structures, resources and external monitoring have the common aim of making the lives of children – already identified as some of the most vulnerable in our society – better' (Department of Health and Children 2009, p. 3). In setting out its many recommendations, the Implementation Plan not only addressed the needs of children in the care of the State's social services, but also included commitments to care, education, health and other specialist services for children deprived of liberty. The *Ryan Report Implementation Plan* was, in fact, a hugely influential document which shaped many of the progressive developments in children's services of the period. For children with the most complex and acute needs, the establishment in 2013 of the Assessment, Consultation and Therapeutic Service (ACTS) under the remit of Tusla, the Child and Family Agency, was a major achievement in providing them with the therapeutic services and supports they need.

Oberstown Children Detention Campus

In line with the strategic direction set out by the *Youth Justice Review* and national policy documents, a substantial programme of reform and investment enabled the establishment of Oberstown Children Detention Campus, as it is now known, as the specialist national facility for the care, education and supervision of all children under 18 years who have been referred by the courts on remand or detention orders. The Children Act, 2001 committed to a child-care model of care for all children in detention, under the supervision of the Director in whose care ('loco parentis') every child is placed, and it established strong governance via a Board of Management with responsibility, on behalf of the Minister for Children, for the management of Oberstown. The Act also provides for annual independent inspection by persons authorised for that purpose, a function currently undertaken by the Health and Information Quality Authority (HIQA). Significantly, when it came to implementing the vision of the *Youth Justice Review*, the Act provided an important framework insofar as s. 158 set out the principal object of Oberstown as providing 'appropriate educational, training and other programmes and facilities' for children referred by a court, 'to promote their reintegration into society' and 'prepare them to take their place in the community as persons who observe the law and are capable of making a positive and productive contribution to society'. Embedding this into the Oberstown approach became a priority and, in 2014, a model of care was adopted to guide all stages of a young person's journey from admission to release, ensuring that their needs were met in a holistic, consistent and multi-disciplinary manner.

The framework, known as CEHOP, is based on the legislative requirement that Oberstown provide children with **C**are, **E**ducation, **H**ealthcare, work on their **O**ffending behaviour and **P**reparation for leaving (Oberstown 2020, p. 10). Implementation of CEHOP involves an integrated and co-ordinated way of working across all Campus staff and services, underpinned by procedures and systems that enable recording and sharing of information. An interagency placement planning process enables the delivery of the CEHOP framework, and multi-disciplinary, clinical meetings are held weekly to identify and review the needs of young people and the services and supports they require (Oberstown 2020, p. 12). Central to the CEHOP is the young person, and the implementation of the Oberstown Participation Strategy, developed in line with the National Strategy on the Participation of Children in Decision-Making, has highlighted the importance of the child being supported to participate in these meetings in an informed and meaningful way (Oberstown 2020, pp 16–8). More recently, Oberstown adopted a Children's Rights Policy Framework, designed to embed rights-based and child-centred approaches into the care children receive, across all areas of need.

The implementation of national strategy to extend the child-centred model of care and education to all children detained by the courts was an extremely challenging process. Multiple internal barriers had to be overcome to replace three disparate detention schools with a single, unified approach, while externally the pressure to accept responsibility for 16- and 17-year-olds from the prison system was understandably strong. While an analysis of the complex process of change is beyond the scope of this chapter, it is clear that a significant role was played by public policy, which set out very clear and consistent expectations for what was to be delivered. Even more important was the leadership provided by the policy-makers involved, whose commitment to ending the use of prison for children, and vision for providing specialist services to children deprived of liberty, among the State's most vulnerable, was steadfast. HIQA's annual reports (2017, 2018, 2019) highlight the significant progress achieved to date in providing the best-possible care to children in Oberstown, in line with the Standards and Criteria for Children Detention Schools. While improvements continue to be required in the reduction of the use of single separation and in improved record keeping, it is evident that the specialist, multi-disciplinary approach to care is beginning to have a positive effect on the quality of care that children receive (HIQA 2019). Improved advocacy services have also enabled children's voices to be heard (Oberstown 2020), a vital component in the establishment of Oberstown as a rights-based facility dedicated to children's care, in line with the vision set out for many years in public policy.

Challenges that remain

By any analysis, Ireland has made significant progress in the adoption of a wide range of substantial public policy measures designed to improve children's lives and government visibility of their treatment. The establishment of the Department of Children can easily be identified as a game changer in promoting a holistic approach to children's policy, with leadership that was both effective and visionary. The dilution of the Department's remit, with additions of disability, equality and integration, and the abolition of the Youth Justice Service are concerning developments against that backdrop.

Substantial advances have been made in delivering on the national policy priorities in youth justice and detention, and even if this remains work in progress, the direction is set. One particular area in which limited progress has been made is with regard to the interface between the State's 'care' and 'justice' systems. The Children Act is clear that criminal proceedings should not be used solely to provide children with assistance or service needed to care for or protect a child (s. 96) and the Children's Court has the power to request Tusla, the Child and Family Agency, to convene a family welfare conference in respect of such a child (s. 77). Despite these provisions, children in Oberstown continue to present with acute needs, and many have had significant involvement with Tusla prior to their detention (Oberstown 2020, pp 8–9). Research by Carr and Mayock (2019) has highlighted that a small number of children in state care, those with particularly acute needs and with experience of residential care settings, continue to end up in detention, and while the causes are multi-factorial, the research found that systemic factors including the profile of care provision, the prosecution of children in care placements and the responsiveness of the youth justice system to children who have often experienced multiple adversity and previous involvement with the criminal justice system all contribute to the phenomenon. Forde has also highlighted the legislative gap that frustrates efforts to ensure that children leaving detention have a statutory entitlement to aftercare that promotes their successful return to their community (Forde 2014). These issues combined suggest that there is some way to go to ensuring that the child-focused approach meets the needs of all troubled children.

References

Carr, N. and Mayock, P. (2019), *Children and Young People in Care and Contact with the Criminal Justice System*, Dublin: Irish Penal Reform Trust.

Commission to Inquire into Child Abuse (2009), *The Report of the Commission to Inquire into Child Abuse*, Dublin: Stationery Office.

Dáil Select Committee on Crime: Juvenile Crime, its Causes and its Remedies (1992), Dublin: The Oireachtas.

Department of Health and Children (2009), *Report of the Commission to Inquire into Child Abuse, 2009*, Implementation Plan, Dublin: Stationery Office.

Department of Justice, Equality and Law Reform (2006), *Youth Justice Review*, Dublin: Stationery Office.

Department of Justice and Equality (2013), *The National Youth Justice Action Plan 2014–2018*, Dublin: Stationery Office.

Expert Group on Children Detention Schools (2006), *First Progress Report to Mr Brian Lenihan, TD, Minister for Children*.

Forde, L. (2014), 'Aftercare for Young People Leaving Care and Detention', *Irish Law Times* vol. 32, no.12, pp 180–84.

Health Information and Quality Authority (HIQA) (2019), *Report of Oberstown Children Detention Campus*, Dublin: HIQA.

Irish Youth Justice Service (2008), *National Youth Justice Strategy 2008–2010*, Dublin: Stationery Office.

Kilkelly, U. (2006), *Youth Justice in Ireland*, Dublin: Irish Academic Press.

Kilkelly, U., and Forde, L. (2019), *Looking Back at Tackling Youth Crime: Youth Justice Action Plan 2014–2018, A Review of Progress Achieved and Lessons Learned*, unpublished.

Muncie, J. (2008), 'The "Punitive Turn" in Juvenile Justice: Cultures of Control and Rights Compliance in Western Europe and the USA', *Youth Justice*, vol. 8, no. 2, pp 107–21.

Oberstown Children Detention Campus (2020), *Annual Report 2019*, Dublin: Oberstown Children Detention Campus.

Office of the Minister for Children and Youth Affairs (2009), *Report of the Commission to Inquire into Child Abuse 2009 Implementation Plan*, Dublin: Stationery Office.

O'Sullivan, E., and O'Donnell, I. (2012), *Coercive Confinement in Ireland: Patients, Prisoners and Penitents*, Manchester: Manchester University Press.

Sargent, P. (2014), *Wild Arabs and Savages. A History of Juvenile Justice in Ireland*, Manchester: Manchester University Press.

PART III

The Citizen and the State – Policy, Governance and Engagement

CHAPTER 6

A New Holy Grail? The Search for Coherence in Public Policy in Ireland

Dermot McCarthy

Introduction

In this chapter, I set out some reflections on the broad challenges to public policy and administration and draw some insights into the search for coherence and consistency, as well as effectiveness, in the policy process.

Background

The modern democratic state is founded on the rule of law and institutions of government that are accountable to the people. The powers of government run wide and deep, but they are constrained in what and how they may do. These powers have developed in line with the expectation of citizens that the state holds ultimate responsibility for their security and, within parameters which are contested, their wellbeing. The state monopoly on the legitimate use of force and the raising of taxes has its counterpart in the expectation that state capacity and public resources will be used to manage the economy so as to deliver high rates of employment at decent incomes, to secure a distribution of income that sustains some minimal level of dignity for all, and ensures access to an adequate volume and quality of public services to meet society's expectations.

The following pages seek to describe the approaches that have been developed to promote consistency and coherence. The challenges and limitations applying in each case are discussed, but there is no attempt to evaluate their impact or their overall effectiveness. There are, however, some pointers towards ways of organising the business of government to reflect more appropriately and, perhaps, more honestly the imprecise and highly contingent nature of the policy-making process and the necessarily experimental nature of what often passes for settled policy.

Foundational roots of coherence

Just as the institutions of government reflect the impact of history, so they also reflect the culture and values of society shaped by that history. The civic culture and the values it embodies exercise a profound influence on the business of government. To the extent that they are widely shared, they provide the reflexive ecosystem within which policies are formulated and services are delivered. These values include expectations of the appropriate role and limits of the state, the distinctive features of communal life to be supported and protected, and the sources of material wellbeing to be nurtured and developed. The more homogenous the society, the more likely the civic culture is to be a forceful and consistent influence on public policy.

Economic conditions exert their influence through cultural expression. The largely peasant agrarian economy and demographically lopsided population of the early years of the State made it unsurprising that citizens would turn to a form of religious expression which echoed and rationalised the harsh circumstances of daily life.

Administrative culture is one aspect of the prevailing political culture. While incorporating the foundational values prevailing in the wider society, it has particular features reflecting the role played by the organisations and individuals charged with supporting the elected government and implementing its policies. This administrative culture extends to norms regarding adherence to law and regulation, tolerance or otherwise for petty corruption, the expectation of uniformity or variations based on the exercise of discretion, and the bias towards conservative rule-following or creative problem-solving.

Ireland has been fortunate in the generally high standards of probity of its officials, but commentators have consistently highlighted a weakness in the exercise of foresight, in contrast with the energy and effectiveness of responses to emergencies. As the structure of the economy and society has changed rapidly over recent decades, it would not be surprising were the administrative culture to lag in its adaptation to changed conditions. This may be reflected in the composition of the public service, as it ceases to reflect the full range of contemporary Irish society, or in its deployment of new technology, or in its understanding of the dynamics of changed social patterns. The need for change has found expression in the introduction of explicit programmes of public service reform over recent decades.

As society and the public service have become more diverse, with more complex needs and demands, so the coherence of policy and administration could no longer rely on instinct and reflex. Instead, explicit provision had to be made for the co-ordination of the efforts of those charged with the business of government. The search for coherence can be found in the adoption, more or less explicitly, of paradigms which express the primary objectives of public policy, with implications that cascade down for individual policy domains and the institutions that support them.

Paradigms that shape policy

Of particular importance is the self-understanding of the Irish State as a small, open economy. Wellbeing depends upon the success of the economy, which in turn requires integration into the international trading order expressed through the European single market.

It is in the area of tax policy that the extent of the influence of this overriding imperative is most evident, with the maintenance of a competitive corporation tax regime as a key priority of Ireland's international policy and a key influence on the structure of the domestic tax system. The locational preferences of overseas investors have also shaped physical planning and development policies, driving population growth in our major cities, and influencing planning policies conducive to their flourishing. Labour-market policies also reflect this priority, with implications for national policies on union recognition and collective bargaining.

A further paradigm which shapes the conduct of public policy is that of the fiscally responsible state. This is consistent with the implications of being a small open economy, but it has its own particular dynamic. It is expressed in the belief that the public finances should be managed so as to secure, on the whole, a fiscal balance where expenditure does not exceed revenue, other than to be applied to productive investments which will generate an economic return to remunerate and ultimately repay the necessary borrowing. These norms are expressed and underpinned by European requirements, and imply that the development of public services is dependent upon the available fiscal space, rather than on the needs of citizens or the ambition of policy-makers. It is a powerful influence on the process of policy-making, beyond the particular institutional arrangements described below.

Another paradigm derived from the small open economy framework is the need for consistency across policy domains if the performance of the economy, expressed in employment and living standards, is to improve on a sustainable basis. First articulated by the National Economic and Social Council (NESC) in the 1980s (NESC 1987), this asserts that the performance of the government in its fiscal management of the state can be successful only if it is matched by the competitiveness of the private sector and underpinned by redistributive arrangements which maintain industrial peace and social harmony. Failure in any one of these domains will frustrate the achievement of the other two. Co-ordination across the social actors whose behaviour is critical to performance and outcomes is therefore required, either through explicit mechanisms, such as those described below, or through some shared understanding and expectations which guide autonomous decision-making. This is, in effect, a description of the social market economy where, through political, market and social channels, each sector must take account of the other and none is able to escape the wider consequences of its own decisions and performance.

Another paradigm which frames expectations of behaviour in Ireland as a liberal democracy aspiring to operate in the social market is the concept of the developmental welfare state (NESC 2005). This is the counterpart to the role of the state in underpinning competitiveness and economic performance. It is an expression of a responsibility of the state to secure the wellbeing of its citizens while, at the same time, respecting the autonomy of markets and the interweaving of social and economic life. It envisages the state as redistributor of resources which ensure income adequacy, without damaging incentives to work and to invest, but delivering this income support in tandem with a variety of services that enable individuals to realise their potential, including those whose physical and other circumstances require public intervention. It is a paradigm which is vulnerable to economic pressures, but it provides a powerful framework for those proposing and designing policies intended to counter disadvantage and enhance the life chances of individuals and communities. It is the framework within which, for example, investment in childcare and early intervention services has attracted support from a wide range of institutions and interest groups.

Against the backdrop of these framing paradigms, the following sections consider the specific procedures and institutional arrangements that have been developed within the public policy system to promote coherence and consistency in the formulation and implementation of policy.

Frameworks and strategies

If paradigms are broad frameworks of understanding which guide priorities and align expectations, frameworks and strategies are the means by which paradigmatic insights are expressed in statements of priority and intent. Having the authority of government, they provide criteria by which governments are willing to hold themselves accountable and by which public bodies can align themselves with the priorities of government.

An important example of such a framework is the Programme for Government, produced by successive Irish governments on their formation. In the case of coalition government, they represent the outcome of negotiation and bargaining by which competing election manifestos are combined, more or less coherently, into a single charter document for a new administration. As political documents, they are permitted a degree of ambition and imprecision which would not generally be acceptable in statements of policy from a government that has commenced its mandate.

Programmes for Government provide clear signals to government departments and agencies as to the priorities that a new government aims to follow and, to some degree, directions as to the steps they will take to pursue the stated objectives. This enables departments and agencies to prepare policy and legislative proposals aligned with the Programme. Conversely, the Programme sends a clear message that it may be fruitless to bring forward proposals in conflict with, or simply not mentioned in, the text. Programmes for Government provide a context and a shaping influence on Statements of Strategy which government departments are legally obliged to publish following the formation of a new government or the appointment of a new minister. The procedure for the preparation of such Statements provides an opportunity for political and administrative oversight from the centre, ensuring that the government's priorities are reflected in the approach and policy commitments of each government department. Departmental Statements of Strategy, in turn, influence the strategic and business planning of the agencies under their aegis. In this way, the directions set in Programmes for Government cascade down through the administrative system to promote a measure of alignment between public institutions.

Programmes for Government do not generally give clear priority rankings for specific measures, nor specify measures to ensure coherence and consistency across the wide-ranging agenda for action. However, governments can, on their formation or subsequently, produce clear statements of priority or guiding principles which will inform their actions. An example is the principles that were proposed by the Government to the social partners in January 2009, following the financial crash of 2008. These gave a clear direction to the shape of budgetary policy, indicating what would and would not be acceptable. These principles were restated and amplified in the National Recovery Plan 2011–14, which provided the framework for the subsequent agreement with the European institutions governing the financial assistance they provided. This Plan, and the subsequent agreement with the Troika, gave granular programmatic detail of the steps which would be taken to restore fiscal balance, through both the curtailment of expenditure and the increase in revenue from a widened tax base. This gave unusual and perhaps unwelcome clarity to departments and agencies as to what would be expected of them over the period of recovery.

Another category of framework document is the form of agreement with the social partners which was entered into by governments over the years from 1987 until 2009. In these wide-ranging agreements, governments undertook to pursue agreed priorities and implement specific measures in the context of commitments to shared goals and consistent behaviour on the part of the social partners, principally through the income policies contained in the associated pay agreements. These partnership agreements were, in each case, negotiated following the adoption of strategic reviews by the National Economic and Social Council (NESC), whose membership includes representatives of the social partners, senior public servants, and a number of independent experts. Because NESC strategic reviews were focused on economic and social policy outcomes, their conclusions and recommendations were framed by reference to what needed to be done, rather than by the contours of political and administrative structures. As a result, the succeeding social partnership agreements also adopted an outcome-focused logic. By setting out agreed objectives in areas such as unemployment, disadvantaged areas or rural development, these programmes required a cross-government approach to implementation. The oversight arrangements for the implementation of these agreements also required collaboration between departments and agencies in reporting (and defending) progress. These agreements encouraged innovations in policy-making, in the form of cross-departmental strategies targeting specific policy goals, such as the first National Anti-Poverty Strategy, and in implementation mechanisms, such as Area-Based Partnership Companies in designated areas of disadvantage.

Strategies to guide and to bind

It has been a long-standing criticism of the Irish public service that it is too focused on the short term and the reactive, at the expense of the longer term and the proactive. It is no accident that the major initiative for public service reform in this generation was labelled the Strategic Management Initiative. The adoption of a strategic approach within public management was designed to embed disciplines which would strengthen the longer-term perspective and equip public bodies to be more intentional in achieving desired goals. As noted above, these goals were expected to be derived from the priorities of the democratically elected government and, through the choreography of strategic planning across departments and agencies, consistent measures would be taken to achieve these goals in a cost-effective manner.

Strategies have been developed by governments to address a wide variety of policy objectives. Each has the ambition of expressing and then delivering a whole-of-government response to the policy challenge concerned. Strategies have been published in respect of broad policy goals which are inherently cross-cutting and require a holistic perspective, such as climate change or spatial development. These strategies reflect the inherent complexity of the business of government. They also demonstrate that the achievement of policy goals is a matter not just of policy formulation, but also of its implementation — the sequence of steps that will be taken by named institutions and agencies to progress the achievement of policy goals within specified timeframes.

The consequence of the existence of a wide range of strategic frameworks is that individual departments and public bodies have to juggle the implications for their own priorities and actions as they develop their own organisational strategy. Departments now operate within a matrix, where their required contributions to policy objectives driven by other ministers and departments have their counterpart in the commitments from external bodies to their own prioritised areas of responsibility. There is a continuing challenge to maintain a consistent approach and a degree of equilibrium across these many dimensions of policy. There may be a further challenge of inconsistencies between the implications of so many strategies. Some national strategies imply a high level of uniformity of approach across the country; others put a premium on the tailoring of action to local circumstances. Some strategies emphasise the provision of choice and co-responsibility with citizens, others emphasise compliance. In every case, there is a tension between the driving authority of the lead department of a cross-government strategy and the autonomy of each department or agency referenced in a strategy (a tension that is lessened when the lead department is at the centre of government, which is why there are so many calls for the Department of the Taoiseach to lead strategies as a sign of serious political intent). Individual departments and agencies must settle priorities for their own staff and budgets. The weakest strategies are those where the commitments of contributing departments and agencies are vague, the perceived political priority is questionable, and implementation mechanisms permit the contribution of departments and agencies to fade into lip service.

Strategy statements are a snapshot in time of the policy intent of government. Their development and implementation, and ultimately their effectiveness, require this strategic intent to be embodied in concrete measures. This, in turn, requires appropriate processes and structures to provide effective instruments of co-ordination and coherence.

Processes and procedures

Government strategies express the importance of consistency across the structures and domains of public policy and administration for the achievement of the desired outcome. At the heart of that recognition is communication, expressed in routines of consultation.

The requirement to consult in preparing strategies is not confined to consulting other government departments. Departments are required to consult with agencies and public bodies operating under their aegis, just as these bodies, in turn, are required to consult with their parent department. The process of consultation is also required to extend to external stakeholders and to the general public. Typically, submissions are invited through public advertisement. In addition, each department has a network of bodies which are recognised to have a legitimate interest in its areas of responsibility. The traditional social partners have particular standing arrangements for consultation, but the norms of good practice in public consultation extend to offering an inclusive approach to all who may wish to contribute. The energy applied to this process, and the impact of suggestions made in response, is clearly capable of wide variation.

All of the requirements regarding consultation in respect of departmental Statements of Strategy apply also to the development of cross-government policy strategies. These typically are developed with input from consultative or advisory groups which are established to assist in the process. In many cases, these include groups who have advocated for the strategy in question and who bring a measure of operational expertise, as well as political legitimacy, to the process. Regular reporting on implementing the strategy is also required. Such reporting provides an opportunity for further external input, including oversight by the relevant Oireachtas committees, which may result in amendments to the strategy as part of the policy cycle.

Structures to promote co-ordination

Procedures regarding consultation and engagement are the software of policy co-ordination. Through appropriate structures, governments seek to hardwire co-ordination into policy areas which are of particular priority. As the responsibilities of government have broadened and deepened, so the architecture of administration has become more complex and sophisticated. While the Constitution limits to fifteen the membership of the government, legislation enables a larger number of departments to be established, resulting at times in ministers having responsibility for more than one department, one of which may typically be assigned to the direct oversight of a minister of state. A recurring question is: what functions are most appropriately grouped together in the configuration of government departments?

The history of departmental architecture is testament to the fact that some functions are regarded as more easily relocated than others, and so feature in recurring re-combinations of functions. Many of the long-established departments of state have stable, core functions which are synonymous with the responsibilities of the state, such as Foreign Affairs. However, even these core functions have been bracketed with a variety of other responsibilities, from time to time. Trade, for example has been associated both with Foreign Affairs, in recognition of the necessarily international dimension to trade policy, and with Business or Enterprise, as trade is vital for business development. A reconfiguration of functions may be intended to signal a particular policy priority for at least the life of a specific government. The establishment of the Department of Further and Higher Education, Research, Innovation and Science provides a recent example.

The combination of functions in any new structural mix is generally intended to produce better synergies and more consistent co-ordination between policy areas which are seen to be complementary in critical respects. There is an inevitable disruption and delay arising from the complex legal, logistical and personnel impacts of such changes. It is rare for discrete units to move smoothly into alignment with other discrete units, without some dispersal of personnel, resulting in a loss of expertise and tacit knowledge.

A more serious difficulty arises from the fact that the removal of organisational barriers between functional areas that have been freshly combined is matched by the erection of new barriers with the functional areas from which they have been detached. The challenges of co-ordination to be addressed in the new structure are typically replaced by fresh challenges of co-ordination with entities and functions which are now on the other side of a departmental boundary. The boundary question is not confined to central government; agencies which are charged with implementing policy acquire new parent departments as a result of reconfiguration. They may also experience organisational change themselves, if new agencies are established to mirror the new functional responsibilities at central government level. As a result, new departmental boundaries requiring new cross-departmental processes may give rise to similar challenges in the direct delivery of services to the community.

The challenges of pursuing co-ordination through organisational structures can be illustrated by the example of the Department of Children and Youth Affairs, recently re-configured as the Department of Children, Equality, Disability, Integration and Youth. The establishment of a government department that would bring together and elevate the political salience of children's needs was long championed by advocates for children's rights. Their case was that a senior minister, with a seat in cabinet, supported by a department with appropriate resources, would have a transformative effect on policies and services for children. It is manifestly the case that the Department has had a significant impact on policy for children, developing important new strategies, initiating new programmes, and providing sustained high-level political attention on issues relating to children and their wellbeing. However, critical policies and services that affect children remain outside its remit. Key areas such as health, education, income support and housing, as they impact on children, still require a cross-departmental approach.

Policies in respect of children were formerly co-ordinated by a Minister for Children who was not a member of the government (though latterly the holder attended Cabinet meetings) but who was supported by an Office with officials assigned from all government departments with key policy responsibilities in respect of children. It is a matter for judgment as to the extent to which the high-level political authority represented by a separate department has provided greater cross-government co-ordination than a more junior political office, but with direct appointments to, and supporting officials assigned from, a range of government departments. An assessment of questions like this cannot be divorced from the crucial factor of the quality and effectiveness of key individuals, both political and official, who lead and animate the various structures.

No matter how widely drawn the brief of a government department or agency may be, it is inevitable that many of the policy areas and services that are critically important for the achievement of its policy goals will lie outside its control. New departments, no less than those they replace, will continue to face the challenges of cross-departmental co-ordination.

One of the institutional arrangements to support co-operation between, and co-ordination of government departments is the establishment of Cabinet Committees. In the not-too-distant past, Cabinet Committees were regarded as internal processes of Cabinet, requiring the protection of cabinet confidentiality. As a result, they were not publicly acknowledged to exist and were outside any system of external scrutiny. They are now publicly acknowledged as part of the machinery of government and attract a measure of public attention. While they remain outside any specific constitutional or legislative framework, there are well-established norms governing their establishment and functioning.

Cabinet Committees are typically supported by teams of senior officials drawn from the same departments as the ministers who comprise the Committee. Often, but not always, led from the centre, these cross-departmental teams are tasked to ensure that the information required to support political deliberation is provided and that policy questions are teased out to the point where clear political direction is appropriate and possible. Cross-departmental teams of officials can also be established without a specific Cabinet Committee to oversee their work. For example, the Tax Strategy Group prepares and analyses issues, and presents policy options, to inform the annual Budget process.

From policy to implementation

It could be argued that there is no policy unless it has been implemented. Without the means to bring about the intended outcomes, and to deliver the mandated outputs, policy is little more than political rhetoric. The traditional model of rational policy-making envisages a logical sequence of steps, beginning with the identification of problems which require a policy response, moving to the formulation of policy options for decision, then to implementation of policy and delivery of services in line with rules and priorities settled by policy-makers, followed by an evaluation of the impact and effectiveness of policy, resulting, finally, in the revision of policy, with fresh instructions for those responsible for implementation, as the cycle begins again.

While this cyclical model has analytical merit, it bears little resemblance to the policy process observed in practice. The identification and definition of policy problems are heavily influenced by the range of available responses that can be made. The options presented to decision-makers for adoption as policy are constrained by perceptions of political preference and resource availability. Policy goals are rarely so clear, and priorities and eligibility criteria are rarely so explicit, as to remove the need for those implementing policy to develop (sometimes extensive) rules, explicit or implicit, to guide the public officials responsible for implementation. In some cases, the choices that are normally seen as the essence of policy-making are, in fact, dependent upon the decisions and actions of those who are formally concerned only with policy implementation.

The process of implementation is critical for policy coherence, then, both in terms of shaping policies as they emerge from central government, and through the cumulative impact of programmes and services on communities and citizens.

The structures of public administration have developed to support specialisation, expertise and effectiveness, but they present a fragmented response to the life experience of those whose needs they address. While governments struggle to bring about a joined-up delivery of policy and services, the lives of communities and families are lived in an organically joined-up fashion. There is no obscuring the connectedness of the circumstances of individuals, families and communities. However, their interaction with public agencies typically requires them to separate their needs and experiences into discrete units, to reflect the administrative boundaries which have been created on behalf of the state. Unless there is a measure of co-ordination between programmes impacting on the lives of citizens and communities, the effectiveness of each individual policy will be reduced by contradictory or diverging effects of collateral government programmes.

The cross-departmental strategies adopted at central government level require a similar integrating framework for the process of implementation. The search for appropriate and effective procedures and mechanisms of co-ordination lies at the heart of the implementation challenge. Some elements of a co-ordinated approach appear to offer a degree of low-hanging fruit. The complexity of administration, and the specialised brief of individual agencies, may represent less of a problem if there is an easily accessible entry point for citizens to the complex architecture of implementation. Online portals can facilitate citizens to navigate the complexities of public administration if information about services and eligibility criteria is marshalled in an appropriately user-friendly way. Whole-of-government websites, such as gov.ie, provide such a possibility. However, ensuring that accurate and accessible material is easily available on all of the public services relevant to particular needs or difficulties of citizens requires significant expertise in assembling and structuring information in a citizen- or consumer- rather than provider-centric way. The expertise of the Citizens Information Board is extremely valuable in producing such resources, both for its own services, and as a support to those in any agency who advise or support citizens.

A less sophisticated approach to making access easier is to share physical premises as a 'front-of-house' facility for a variety of agencies. Traditionally, post offices and Garda stations have been points of distribution for information and application forms and, to some degree, for processing of applications or confirming eligibility. Even these are under pressure, as the post office network is required to operate more commercially, while gardaí are focused on developing a more professional policing service in line with the report of the Commission on the Future of Policing in Ireland, in part through withdrawing from all non-policing functions.

With limitations on the ease with which citizens can obtain information about, and access to, the multiplicity of public services through streamlined channels, an alternative approach is to facilitate access by agencies to information about citizens, including families and communities, in particular sharing citizens' information between agencies which engage with them. An example is the Public Services Card, which enables identity to be established for the purposes of accessing a wide variety of services and programmes without the need repeatedly to authenticate identity. Similar benefits could be achieved if a standardised means test were applied by different agencies, whereby citizens could have their means assessed once in any relevant period for the purposes of all means-tested services. Unfortunately, however, definitions of means differ between agencies, reflecting the context of their programmes, while the relevant time periods for assessing eligibility can also vary. An alternative approach to information sharing is the provision of access by public agencies to all or some of each other's data concerning individual citizens and families. Legislative provision exists for this to happen in certain circumstances, and there is currently limited access in certain well-defined circumstances. However, there is understandable unease at the risks to privacy and civil liberties which extensive information sharing between public agencies would entail.

The co-ordination of effort in order to deliver on policy priorities is generally pursued at the level of geographical units. However, the geographical dimension is not straightforward; different agencies operate to different spatial units, at regional, county, district or parish level. Statistics and other indicators of activity and need may not be comparable across agencies. The overview available through some agencies may give rise to significant privacy concerns. While such challenges can be met, they require considerable effort and analytical dexterity. Even with full co-operation and usable data, such an overview is necessarily incomplete, since it lacks the perspective of the residents of the community and users of services.

Even successful attempts to share information and analysis represent only a weak form of co-ordination. Agencies are still mandated to deliver particular programmes, often in predetermined ways. Organisational priorities and loyalties place formidable obstacles in the way of the joined-up approach which public policy seeks to achieve. As a result, various mechanisms have been developed to bring about a sustained focus on specific local problems and better co-ordination of effort.

For example, Drugs Task Forces were established to bring together all those concerned with the problem of illegal drug use in well-defined locations. The objective is to take a comprehensive approach to address both the supply and demand sides of the illegal drugs problem. While members of the Garda Síochána are primarily concerned with containing and reducing the supply of illegal drugs, this cannot be divorced from the dynamics of demand at local level, including the role of those suffering from addiction, in local supply chains. Reducing demand for drugs has implications for socio-economic disadvantage at local level, the provision of facilities and activities for young people to improve alternatives to the drug culture, and for locally based treatment and support services for those wishing to overcome their addiction.

Mechanisms such as Local Drugs Task Forces represent a step beyond information sharing. They facilitate consultation and they attempt a measure of co-ordination. However, they have no directive powers and limited budgets with which to incentivise services and operations. A step further along the path to co-ordination is to give lead responsibility to one body or agency to structure and manage complementary services, so as to provide a more integrated response to the needs of communities and families. There have been, for example, a number of attempts to build on the strong relationship between schools and local families. Over the period of the national school cycle, relationships of trust develop between families and schools, grounded in daily interaction. The insights of teachers and other school staff into the developmental needs of children and the capacities of their families present, prima facie, a promising context for developing programmes and services that are tailored to local conditions and family needs. This would include developing accessible childcare and preschool provision, encouraging take-up of appropriate developmental and therapy services, support for parenting, and the provision of access to adult education and counselling, so that a holistic approach to the needs of children and their families could be developed. The potential of such an approach was recognised by the introduction of an Area Based Childhood Programme – the ABC – on a pilot basis (Centre for Effective Services 2013).

An example of a locally integrated approach with statutory powers and dedicated streams of funding was the Dublin Docklands Development Authority (DDDA). Its brief was to secure the wellbeing of the existing Dublin dockside communities as the area underwent transformation, from industrial and port use to office development, and to promote harmony and integration between the different communities within its area. With resources from development levies, and statutory powers to influence physical planning, the DDDA proved remarkably effective. It was wound up and its functions transferred to Dublin City Council, reflecting a view that such integrated approaches are best led by a statutory planning authority operating under the direction of elected public representatives. Similar approaches, with a similar fate, were taken in other regeneration areas in Dublin and Limerick. A variant on this approach to a public body leading integrated development is being pursued in Dublin by the North-East Inner-City Programme Implementation Board, which operates under the aegis of the Department of the Taoiseach, with participation from a variety of statutory agencies and the local community, with funding provided centrally for specific initiatives, and with the opportunity to influence the local budgets and programmes of participating public bodies (NEIC 2021).

It might be wondered why such area-based initiatives were not entrusted from the beginning to the relevant local authority. Indeed, the challenge of co-ordinating the implementation of public policy might be assumed to be entirely appropriate to local government, given its clear geographic remit. In truth, Irish politics and public administration have been generally suspicious of local government. Despite local democratic mandates, local authorities are heavily constrained in the limited areas for which they hold direct responsibility. As planning authorities, they are required to have regard to national guidelines and the directive features of national spatial strategy. With limited exceptions, the revenue available to local authorities is determined centrally. Their role in housing development and sanitary services is also framed by national policy and standards. Their relative lack of autonomy, and the narrow range of services for which they are responsible, are in marked contrast to many European countries. Nevertheless, their overarching responsibility for the physical environment and their capacity to animate community engagement have led to recognition of their convening power in areas like emergency planning and civic life.

The effective co-ordination of public services requires an authority structure with power of direction, at least within certain parameters. Managing the necessary degree of integration across services at local authority level would require a significant planning and evaluation capacity which, on the one hand, might be considered beyond their scope, while, on the other, might be expected to weaken the management of individual services. Furthermore, as political bodies, local authorities would expect to have a policy role which could run counter to policies set at national level.

National authorities may be reluctant to incur that risk by entrusting their services and programmes to local government. Likewise, service providers at local level may be reluctant to cede authority over their activities to local government by recognising any implicit power of direction on the part of local authorities.

In these circumstances, it may not be surprising that innovative structures outside the settled architecture of public administration should have emerged to bring about a measure of integration. Such initiatives have the added merit of facilitating the participation of voluntary and community bodies, which play a large role in the delivery of social services in Ireland. Indeed, the earliest attempts at creating structures of co-ordination at local level were Social Service Councils, established in the 1970s at the initiative of local voluntary bodies (Limerick Social Service Council 2020).

Organisations of this type, of which Family Resource Centres are the most numerous at present, effectively act as brokers of services, mediating between public agencies and the communities they serve. One organisation of this type has reported that it delivers a suite of eleven programmes or services, with financial support from eight different public bodies (St Andrew's Resource Centre 2020). Because these services are managed together, and delivered from the same premises, and because the relevant staff co-operate with each other in the planning and delivery of services, they have opportunities to combine and tailor services to the particular needs of families and individuals. Those who approach the organisation for one purpose can be guided and accompanied to access other services, which may address other needs. By virtue of their overview of family and community circumstances, such organisations are well placed to innovate in service design, and to seek community and philanthropic support to go beyond the parameters of publicly funded services.

There are also economies of scale in the operation of premises, transport and administrative support which make local delivery more cost-effective than if each service or programme looked to a separate structure to support its operations. Models of this kind are not without challenge: issues of client confidentiality and privacy need to be respected in strong protocols. Staff delivering services need support and supervision, and to be strongly networked into external professional and provider groups to support standards and stimulate new thinking. Organisations may struggle with the requirements and expectations of external funding bodies, especially when they entail diverging requirements in respect of records and reporting, or style of operation. There is, inevitably, the difficulty of uneven coverage by such bodies. Organisations like Family Resource Centres require local initiative and capacity to establish and maintain them. Communities which might benefit most from such interventions may not have that capacity, or the support of public agencies for funding. Nevertheless, this approach provides the most encouraging example of integrated service delivery, whereby the interaction between separate policies and programmes, for good or bad, is taken explicitly into account through focusing on the perspective of the citizen or consumer (Tusla Child and Family Agency 2020).

Conclusion

This chapter has reviewed the complexities of pursuing coherence and consistency in the formulation and implementation of public policy. It is self-evident that conflicting policy goals and inconsistent implementation procedures frustrate the achievement of the public good which state institutions exist to promote. Tackling such problems may require a re-statement of policy objectives, so as to resolve inconsistencies by adopting a clear set of priorities. It may also require revised eligibility and operating rules, so that inconsistencies are eliminated. It is most likely, however, that tensions between policy goals and different organisational requirements will continue to frustrate the ideal of an integrated approach across the relevant areas of public policy and administration. The search for the Holy Grail of joined-up government is unlikely to be successfully concluded. The search is worthwhile, however, because progress can be made. An abiding focus on coherence is a powerful instrument of policy-learning.

Pursuing better integration requires recognising the inbuilt centripetal forces – values, norms and traditions which underpin political and administrative culture, and the centrifugal forces – specialisation, organisational and professional boundaries, and the pursuit of institutional and personal power and autonomy, which shape policy and administration. Channelling these forces in a more productive direction at central government level has led to the adoption of strategic policy frameworks, the development of procedures, and the creation of institutional mechanisms to support greater coherence and consistency.

The critical importance of implementation for the achievement of intended goals is now widely recognised as a route to better linkages between policies. This chapter has reviewed initiatives to that end and the challenges that they face. The most potent driver of integration is the lived experience of the communities, families and individual citizens whose wellbeing is the object of public action. The more policy and administration are considered in the light of the needs of the intended beneficiaries, the more likely the potential for co-ordination and integration will be recognised.

It is clear that consultation between state providers is a necessary, but weak, form of cohesion. Mechanisms to co-ordinate the efforts of separate agencies are well-meaning, but often falter. The search for integrated delivery offers the best option for achieving the elusive hope of a joined-up response to citizens' needs. Given the history of Irish administration, and the sheer weight of tradition embodied in its structures, it may be that the route to effective integration lies outside the bureaucratic structures of the administrative state. The example of Family Resource Centres points to the potential of organisations acting as brokers between communities and public authorities, bundling together packages of services tailored to the needs of those they serve, informed by intimate knowledge of their clients, and easily accessible to them. The active promotion of such integrating structures at local level would take public administration beyond a frustrating search for co-ordination towards mechanisms to achieve actual integration, with capacity for informing policy as well as improving administration.

One important additional factor in achieving coherence and integration is the personal commitment of those in key positions in the system of policy formulation and implementation. A personal commitment to doing the best for our citizens, and a vision of change inspired by that goal, can be powerful drivers of change. Leadership that is courageous and wise can mobilise energies and motivate challenges to settled practice.

References

Centre for Effective Services (CES) (2013), *The Area Based Childhood Programme 2013–2017*, www.effectiveservices.org.

Children and Young People's Services Committees (2020), Overview of CYPSCs 2019, www.cypsc.ie

Constitution of Ireland, The (1937), Dublin: Government Publications, Article 28.4.2.

Department of Education (1965), *Investment in Education*, Stationery Office: Dublin.

Department of the Taoiseach, *Cabinet Handbook*, www.gov.ie

Limerick Social Service Council (2020), *Annual Report 2019*, www.lssc.ie.

National Economic and Social Council (NESC) (1987), *A Strategy for Development 1986–1990*, Dublin: NESC.

National Economic and Social Council (NESC) (2005), *The Developmental Welfare State*, Dublin: NESC.

North East Inner City (NEIC) Programme Implementation Board (2021), *Annual Report 2020*, www.neic.ie.

Sabel, Charles (1996), *Ireland: Local Partnerships and Social Innovation*, Paris: OECD.

St Andrew's Resource Centre (2020), *Annual Report 2019*, Dublin: St Andrew's Resource Centre.

St Ultan's School, Integrated Care and Education, www.stultans.ie.

Tusla Child and Family Agency (2020), *The Family Resource Centre Programme*, Dublin: Tusla.

CHAPTER 7

CONSULTATION OR PARTNERSHIP? WHAT ROLE FOR CIVIL SOCIETY IN POLICY DEVELOPMENT?

Mary Murphy

Introduction

This chapter reflects on the changing policy role of Irish civil society over the last forty years. Having assessed past achievements and limitations regarding policy development, it looks forward and asks what value civil society might add to policy development in Ireland. We first define civil society and the particular Irish nomenclature of 'community and voluntary sector', distinguishing between community and voluntary actors, on the one hand, and service and advocacy-oriented actors, on the other, and observing how dual processes of austerity and marketisation have reinforced the service orientation of civil society in Ireland. Two key lenses, participation and knowledge, are then used to reflect on the achievements and limitations of the community and voluntary sector over the years of social partnership and subsequently. Taking participation first, we reflect on the power dynamics in policy development, between the state and the sector, and within the sector, and ask to what degree 'participation' or 'access' reflected policy influence. We observe gendered power dynamics within and across state and society actors. We then reflect on power as knowledge, asking whether and how what is understood as evidence in policy development changed over time, whether what constitutes evidence might change again, and how this might impact on the role and power of civil society in policy development.

We conclude by looking forward and asking what role civil society might play in tackling the wicked problems of the third decade of the twenty-first century. New forms of power and new forms of participation offer civil society new ways to engage in change and transformation. The state, in responding to these new forms of power and participation, will increasingly find that neither traditional and hierarchical forms of consultation nor partnership will meet a more horizontal form of civil society. The future role of civil society in policy development needs to be enabled by meaningful processes of co-creation and co-production that not only empower but also recognise and validate various forms of knowledge for policy.

Civil society in Ireland

Civil Society in Ireland – the Community and Voluntary Sector (CVS)

In Ireland, the term Community and Voluntary Sector (CVS) has traditionally represented what in European terms is more often called 'civil society' (CS), and what are sometimes referred to in academic and policy literature as Non-Governmental Organisations (NGOs). While the term 'civil society' is contested, it is most often used to refer to the space outside the family, market and state, and so includes organised and grassroots groups, including NGOs, social movements, trade unions, grassroots and local community organisations and faith groups. Many see CS as a democratic necessity, an arena where people network, socialise, exchange ideas, and mobilise or campaign on issues of shared concern (Chaney 2020). This understanding posits CS as a watchdog of democracy, counterbalancing the power of the state (Rees Jones et al. 2020). While we often theoretically assume a unified CS, this is not upheld in reality. In seeking power to influence, CS is also vulnerable to the corrupting influence of power, and can be co-opted, dominated and subverted by other actors including the state, market and societal actors. CS in Ireland and elsewhere is not united, rather it is diverse and can be a conflictual space. We are not 'all in this together', not all actors are equal in resources and access to power, while in a pluralist society CS can and does promote contested values, which reinforce less democratic norms, including racism and patriarchy.

In Ireland, the language of 'community' and 'voluntary' reflects the important contributions of different traditions, ideologies and models of change over the history of the Irish State, and reflect the contemporary diversity within CS in Ireland. The last century has seen a growth in the range and type of organisations found in the CVS in Ireland, with a clear shift from a church-dominated CVS to a more diverse range of voluntary and professional groups, both large and small. Benefacts (2018) estimates that at least 29,000 non-profit organisations represent 11 per cent of all organisations in Ireland. Visser (2019) argues this is likely underestimated. Much CVS activity is driven by volunteering and service-provision-type activities, including sport, culture and charity. Political or policy engagement has always been present in the shape of social movements that often conflicted with the state, but CS also existed in a subservient, clientalistic, political culture where voluntary services often operated 'in the shadow of the state' (Murphy 2011, p. 170). From the 1970s onwards, often funded by the EU, community-development-oriented organisations have challenged this culture. While community is primarily understood as a geographical space, it has also come to be understood as community of interest (for example, lone parents or Travellers). Over time, community-development-led processes generated greater capacity for policy engagement. Grounded in people's experience of poverty and exclusion, a structural analysis of inequality informed policy development and debate.

Neither policy development nor policy influencing are linear. CVS actors are diverse in size, shape and scope. Neither uniform nor static, CVSs vary considerably in their model of change and, over time, are shaped by, and also shape, de-democratisation and re-democratisation of public policy processes. The past thirty years were first dominated by two decades of social partnership (1986–2008). The most recent decade (2009–2020) was framed at one end by austerity, with the mid-period seeing a period of New Politics, which brought new political opportunity structures for CVS participation in policy development, and the latter end of the decade has been dominated by the COVID-19 pandemic. Particularly since the 2008 crisis, services traditionally delivered by the CVS have been opened up to market actors, and advocacy restrictions ('gag clauses') are now common in service-delivery agreements, limiting CVS policy capacity and activity (Harvey 2014). Likewise, austerity has fundamentally altered both capacity and the infrastructure within which CVS actors engage in policy development. As the Advocacy Coalition observed, there is often a false distinction between service and advocacy, with many service organisations engaging in forms of self-advocacy, and with multiple forms and levels of individual, societal and transformational advocacy (Walsh et al. 2013). However, many key organisations have had to prioritise service provision over policy analysis, engagement or advocacy, leading to a significant loss of capacity for 'social documentation' (Harvey 2020).

An example of the ups and downs of service-delivery-informed policy development and advocacy is offered in Harvey's (2020) insightful reflection on Ireland's national programme of 121 city-, town- and rural-based Family Resource Centres (FRCs) which support children, families and communities, especially those disadvantaged. First emerging in Ireland in the context of community-development-informed policy in the 1970s, they were consolidated as a Family Resource Centre Programme in 1994. The FRCs were badly damaged by austerity; budgets fell 30 per cent from €18.84 million to a low point of €13.09 million, and, despite high levels of social distress and increased demand on services, were never restored to pre-2008 levels. These budget reductions led to radical cuts in staffing, with remaining services focused on survival and 'an environment inimical to fresh thinking'. Funding for social documentation virtually collapsed, the analysis from FRC work and their acquired knowledge was not articulated in policy development. This led to gaps in arguments for 'social reconstruction' and over-reliance on theories of the English-speaking world (tending towards individualised analysis over structural disadvantage). FRCs' services remain delivered through community development principles, delivering low or no-cost, trusted, local, accessible services. FRCs demonstrated flexibility and adaptability, playing a strategic part in the delivery of local supports during the pandemic. However, to be transformational and policy focused, the FRC needs to be sufficiently resourced, with capacity to generate and disseminate grounded documentation and evidence. Without such investment, it is difficult to foster an innovative environment conducive to forward development, and to maximise opportunities strategically, to utilise the accumulated FRC knowledge in policy development.

Achievements and limitations of the CVS in policy development

This section first reflects on the changing role of the CVS from the mid-1980s to the late 2000s, when Ireland operationalised national and local partnership as an innovative form of networked governance. It then considers the past decade and how and whether the CVS has innovated new forms of policy development. Rather than focus on policy content, we focus on what can be learned about power, first as seen through the lens of participation and the relationship between civil society and the state, and then through the lens of knowledge as power.

Participation as power: civil society and the state

From 1993, the CVS began to participate in a range of social partnership institutions, including the National Economic and Social Forum (NESF) and the National Economic and Social Council (NESC), where it still retains representation. A comprehensive reflection on the C+Vs Pillars (CVP) engagement in a quarter century of some or other form or social partnership or dialogue is beyond the scope of this chapter. Some achievements are obvious, but so too are limitations. The eight rungs on Arnstein's (1969) ladder of citizen participation usefully remind us that not all forms of participation are positive; some lower forms can be manipulative or at best tokenistic, while other forms of participation can be meaningful, leading to real power and input into decision-making.

While some posit CVS engagement in social partnership institutions as a positive form of deliberative democracy, or an extension and widening of participatory democracy, others see it as an unequal participation that effectively co-opted or smothered civil society in the embrace of the state (Murphy 2002). Positive assessments of participation sometimes confuse or conflate access and influence. The reality of much of social partnership participation was uneven access to power. Participation of many smaller and less powerful groups in the 26-member Community Platform was mediated through a smaller number of more powerful actors in the Community and Voluntary Pillar (CVP). Larragy (2014) draws attention to the asymmetric nature of power, where CVP actors are less powerful than other social partners (business, trade union and agriculture). Murphy (2002) warned of a less benign 'illusion of consensus' that shielded from sight the inequality embedded in the process of participation, which also generated and legitimated unequal distributional outcomes. Some worried about the capacity of such mechanisms to smother civil society in the embrace of the state (Meade 2005), or more forcefully to asphyxiate or choke civil society, co-opting it and diverting its leadership from other more effective forms of influencing and advocacy (Harvey 2020). The structures and processes of social partnership have been critiqued from the perspective of parliamentarians who not only questioned the power of civil servants who brokered national social partnership programmes, but who were less than complimentary about the unrepresentative 'motley crew' who comprised the CVP. Indeed, Arnstein (1969) had noted the difficulties of organising a representative and accountable citizens' group in the face of futility, alienation, and distrust: conflict is inevitable if real power is at stake.

Figure 1: Ladder of Participation

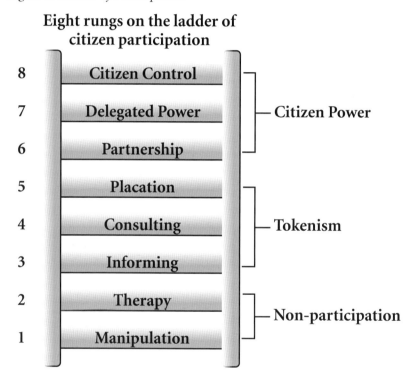

Source: Arnstein 1969

Social partnership was a 'gendered institution' where most key roles and power were held by men, in the civil service, in the supporting institutions, and in each social partner Pillar. That said, feminist forms of enabling leadership were also in evidence. During the period 1994–2004, a core group of female civil servants rose to power through departmental promotion. These represented the first of a new cohort of women in senior roles – Assistant Secretary-General, and above – who were the first generation of female leaders to emerge after the marriage bar. It has been documented elsewhere how these women supported each other in an overwhelmingly male environment. Some in the CVS also experienced a form of enabling power, exercised by some senior civil servants, many of them women, who sought to nurture female leadership. Some of these women quietly enabled key actors (many of them women, including the author) in the C+V sector, advising, nudging, and supporting them to make key interventions, to take strategic steps, pointing to alternative routes, and generally encouraging them along the way. Within the C+V Pillar, a relatively conscious form of parallel leadership emerged where women supported and enabled each other (even when their respective individual organisations clashed). Much was learned through quiet leadership – for example, use of the opportunity of an underspend in European Social Funding to mainstream childcare in that fund, and the subsequent establishment of a High-Level Group on Childcare, opening up space for the subsequent framing of childcare as a public problem requiring state investment and institutional responses.

Post 2008, the remnants of social partnership have limped on in a form of 'social dialogue', including the National Economic Dialogue and pre-budget consultations. While the CVP still clings to such nomenclature and participates in the remaining institutions, many CVSs have also sought to find new forms of participation and power and ways to influence policy and practice. They do so, however, in the context of austerity and a political environment that has eroded policy capacity within the CVS. Over the period 2010–2013, the CVS experienced a dramatic fall in funding of up to 35 per cent, and a related loss of employment of 11,150 jobs, eroding policy capacity of that sector (Murphy and O'Connor 2021). Over the same period, there was a relatively hostile political environment for advocacy, as the state suppressed or inhibited some advocacy, while also supporting other forms of advocacy (Harvey 2014). In particular, a number of social and equality institutions were closed, merged or scaled back. As Harvey (2020) argues, the impact of the dissolution of the institutions should not be underestimated and is still experienced over the long term as well as the medium and short term. It meant a definable loss in skills, advice, documentation and knowledge in the field, and translated into a 'weak community infrastructure' and loss of social capital on a significant scale.

Just as striking is the loss of social policy capacity of the state. There has been a considerable reduction in the points of engagement, with the closure of the Combat Poverty Agency particularly impacting on the range of supports and the formal/informal networking opportunities within a previously rich poverty, inclusion and equality infrastructure. The range of state agencies in the social policy field that were disbanded is striking, and also dismayed key civil servants and political or policy actors who had for decades championed their establishment. They ranged from the National Crime Council to the National Consultative Committee on Racism and Interculturalism; Education Disadvantage Committee; Centre for Early Childhood Development and Education; National Council on Ageing and Older People; Women's Health Council; Children Acts Advisory Board; Crisis Pregnancy Agency; Affordable Homes Partnership; Centre for Housing Research; the Homeless Agency; National Economic and Social Forum; Office for Active Citizenship; Library Council; and Comhar (Harvey 2012).

Post 2008, however, we also see investment in, and innovation of, new forms of policy development. These new institutions offer a different type of vehicle for the CVS to engage in policy development. At a time of declining trust in all institutions (Edelman 2020), such initiatives endeavour to engage citizens more directly in political processes, by either widening and/or deepening participation and placing the citizen at the heart of policy. Harris (2021) notes that Irish innovations to facilitate public consultation, participation and deliberation, in the form of Citizens' Assemblies (CAs), are now broadly accepted as a way of doing politics. In channelling citizen involvement into policy development, such institutions have some potential to replace civil society as the traditional conduit for participation in policy development. That said, there are clear examples of the capacity of the CVS to influence concrete policy outcomes through new policy processes. The Citizens' Assembly on the Eighth Amendment was perhaps the clearest example of how a participative process was used to generate an innovative approach to an old problem, and to reframe the policy approach to reproductive rights and abortion In Ireland. Organisations like the National Women's Council informed the process and deliberations (Murphy and O'Connor 2021). The Citizens' Assembly on Climate Change is also associated with increasing policy momentum, and benefited from the active input of environmental NGOs (Harris 2021). Notably such processes have not successfully influenced issues of socio-economic distribution, and these new forms of participation have yet to demonstrate that they can enable those currently excluded from the political and economic processes to be meaningfully included. Mechanisms for a redistribution of power are needed for significant social reform which can share the benefits of an affluent society (Arnstein 1969, p. 216).

Knowledge as power: New forms of knowledge

Knowledge is another form of power. It is important to analyse the achievements and limitations of social partnership from the perspective of capacity to contest dominant understandings and framing of societal problems and to influence alternative ways to understand the range of potential policy responses. Over the period in question (the early 1990s to 2008), the policy capacity of the state grew considerably, as did the infrastructure and capacity to gather and analyse data. This reflected an essential underpinning of the international shift to 'evidence-based policy', or 'evidence-informed policy' (Ruane 2021), or more cynically 'policy-informed evidence'. Here the CVS experienced both opportunity and threat. The threat was evident in how policy language and discourse became more mechanistic as econometrics became privileged as a more dominant form of communication (Dukelow 2021). This left many CVS interests struggling, where particularly smaller CVS actors, often working with or representing more vulnerable communities, found themselves ill-equipped to participate meaningfully, with consequences for what would become more uneven power dynamics within the Community and Voluntary Pillar (CVP).

The opportunity, which in some respects many failed to grasp, was the degree to which the CVP was well placed to translate its relatively unique experiential knowledge into the policy process. Civil servants and politicians intuitively understand that this knowledge is a necessary part of policy formation and especially implementation (they do not, however, always seek or listen to this form of knowledge). Indeed, rather than representational roles or justification of participation on the basis of associational or participative democracy, the CVS participation was more often valued, at least in theory, for the expert or experiential knowledge that the CVS might bring to the table; in effect, capacity to contribute to the policy puzzle was what really legitimated CVS participation. At times, CVS expert experiential knowledge did reframe knowledge – for example, in relation to social welfare benchmarking and indexation, unemployment and child poverty. New understandings emerged as to how childcare might be organised, how institutions worked from the perspective of the end-user, and how an inadequate rural transport infrastructure translated into social exclusion.

O'Donnell (2021) observes how a different quality of knowledge can be created when institutional mechanisms enable actors to stretch the boundaries of traditional organisational structures. He describes how the NESC in the 1990s used processes of multi-actor, multi-level engagement to 'puzzle' about emerging challenges. This led to framing and reframing to create 'a series of common knowledge events' – the 'inner workings of co-operation' creatively achieved some degree of consensus and 'new shared understanding'. However, despite some innovative experimentation, not all such mechanisms were inclusive, and the appropriate actors were not always found in the appropriate spaces. Those who have worked most closely with those experiencing marginalisation and exclusion often relate how neither the workers' nor the service-users' voices or experiences influenced how problems are understood or framed. McCarthy (2021, p. xxi) highlights 'the importance of officials, analysts and activists who have direct experience of the lived experience of those who are the focus of policy, but who are also fluent in the language of formal policy development, a rarer combination than might be supposed'. Sylda Langford stood out as a civil servant who brought such grounded experiences into policy processes that led to real improvements in the position of vulnerable children and disadvantaged people in Ireland. It is somewhat ironic that the demands of participation in national and local partnership governance often drew leaders away from the everyday and local work of their organisation, loosening their grip on experiential knowledge of workers, members and service-users. We noted above the case study of the Family Resource Centres, where austerity had all but eroded capacity for social documentation and for translating experiential knowledge into policy development. In anticipating how to resolve future wicked problems associated with extreme marginalisation, we need to be cognisant of the intersectional perspectives of the 17 per cent of the population not born in Ireland.

Austerity was heavily gendered in its impact, with particular consequences for diluting the policy capacity of women's organisations who had to prioritise declining resources for service delivery. A disproportionate number of women-focused national agencies were closed, merged or scaled back, with significant consequences for the strategic role gender expertise can play in policy analysis and change. Cullen (2021) identifies that gender policy analysis requires the expertise to apply gender as a variable in the range of processes that generate policy analysis. This is seen in gender audits, gender budgeting, research and analysis, gender consultation, gender training, and gender assessments. Capacity for all of this was diminished in the context of austerity, which also had the effect of leaving gendered impacts of austerity less visible. A further consequence of austerity was the delayed development of gender disaggregated data, much needed for policy analysis, the absence of which continues to hinder policy analysis capacity in, for example, unemployment, homelessness, violence against women, and gender budgeting. Resistance to adopting gendered analysis demonstrates how inhospitable some contexts are to this form of knowledge and how policy institutions and actors shape capacity for gendered policy.

Harris (2021) argues that deliberative democratic innovation in the shape of Citizens' Assemblies can, as a process of co-design, engage citizens in the systematic analysis of policy problems in ways that are inclusive, evidence based, transparent and accountable. The role of the expert committee and expert presenter in framing what is known about a particular policy in participative and deliberative processes like Citizens' Assemblies raises the critical question of who decides what knowledge informs debate, and whose knowledge gets heard in policy development. From an academic perspective, Dukelow (2021) observes a more critical turn in social policy analysis and scholarship, and a notable turn to valuing the lived experience and its relevance to policy-making. Likewise, we also see, through the learned experience of narratives and storytelling in referendums, the insistence on personal stories as part of the framing of issues in both the Climate Change and the Gender Equality Citizens' Assemblies, suggesting a respect for and interest in experiential and qualitative knowledge often undervalued by experts.

Post 2011, and particularly post 2016, a 'new politics has emerged that is characterised by new parliamentary and public forms of policy-making that require new forms of policy analytical capacity with different implications for the CVS. There are more abundant opportunities to liaise with the political system including parliamentary committees, to engage in setting agendas, framing narratives, collaborating and networking with more diverse actors (Connaughton 2021). The emergence of the Parliamentary Budget Office is welcome from the perspective of the CVS which has traditionally tried to influence budget policy through the old, tired formula of the Pre-Budget Submission. There is also more discussion of budget proofing. Gender and equality budgets have played a role elsewhere in generating social change (Murphy 2017).

Discussion

Power has always been a contested concept, as have been the concepts of consultation, participation, partnership and knowledge. Timms and Heimans (2018) argue that a new form of power is changing the twenty-first century. This is less related to old institutions and forms of decision-making and more about a hyperconnected world where ideas and movements spread with speed and with power to shape the future. Offering international examples of #MeToo and Black Lives Matter, they argue that a new form of horizontal power now exists, where the capacity to produce intended effects is no longer the preserve of 'old power' in traditional institutions that are closed and relatively inaccessible. The 'new power', they argue, is open, participatory and peer driven. It works less in institutions and more as an energy, or a surge in channels. Old power values of formal governance, exclusivity, confidentiality, professionalism and longevity are contested by new values of informality, collaboration, sharing, openness and transparency, conditional affiliation and participation. Crucially, participation itself takes new forms – it is less recognisable in Arnstein's ladder or continuum of participation, which reflected three hierarchical tiers (symbolic consultation, tokenistic participation and citizen power or partnership). Rather, they offer citizens and civil society a 'participation scale' where, on the lowest ranks, old power participative behaviours are limited to traditional compliance or consumption, while new power behaviours enable sharing, affiliation, adapting, funding, producing and shaping (Timms and Heimans 2018, p. 71).

While they offer no Irish examples, we see local examples in Together for Yes, Fridays for Future, and Irish responses to Black Lives Matter. Looking forward, what consequences will such new power behaviours have both for the state and civil society and for future forms of participation and knowledge formation? Arguably, shifting forms of power and patterns of citizen participation offer civil society new ways to engage in change and transformation. This will likely shift how key actors engage with governance mechanisms and will also require civil society to reimagine its own traditional organisational structures. The state, in responding to these new forms of power and participation, will find that neither traditional and hierarchical forms of consultation nor partnership will meet a more horizontal form of civil society.

Rather, the future role of civil society in policy development needs to be enabled by meaningful processes of co-creation and co-production that not only empower but also recognise and validate various forms of knowledge for policy. Murphy and Hogan (2020) argue that this is particularly the case in the context of the scale of change and adaption that will be required of state civil society and citizens in the context of climate transition. We already see how localised and inclusive responses to climate adaption and transition need to be. The pandemic has illustrated how existing mechanisms are limited in their representation and related capacity to understand the needs of key vulnerable groups and to enable new forms of inclusive participation. Tackling future problems requires new forms of new and old local experiential knowledge, and new mechanisms to generate and share knowledge. These require an openness to new processes that are less formal and institutionalised than previous participative experiments or forms of social partnership. Adaptability requires that we find innovative (and honest) ways to retire institutions that are tired or are less relevant (Murphy and Hogan 2020).

New types of collaboration and consultation are imagined in the concepts of co-production[1] and co-creation, and recognise the need for the service-user to engage in policy design and implementation. Implementing this scale of change in values and behaviours will undoubtedly require new and complex skills, reflexivity and innovation from all actors (Torfing et al. 2019; Voorberg et al. 2015). Nonetheless, Ireland has some experience in 'co-production'; to differing degrees, this principle informed the model of network governance or social partnership in Ireland (O'Donnell 2021). Likewise, examples exist in Ireland and elsewhere and offer promising new ways of enabling policy to be more inclusive and better able to meet its goals. Choice-based models of social services, for example, often provide better outcomes and are cost-effective (Healy and Clarke 2020). New and imaginative forms of participation include the Practice and Participation of Rights, innovative forms of local participation such as participatory budgeting and Citizens' Assemblies. However, all of these are challenged to be inclusive in the context of economic and educational inequality. Forms of racism and stigmatising practices create barriers to inclusive policy analysis in both state and civil society. Sabel (2020) recognises that the need for a continual process of adaption requires that all actors, including civil society, but also national and local statutory actors, continually adapt and acquire the skills and values to enable more engaged forms of horizontal and local participation. In conclusion, the future role for civil society in policy development lies in neither consultation nor partnership, but in new innovative forms of participation and knowledge production.

---

1 Co-production denotes the '*active involvement* of end-users' as partners in various stages of the design, management, and delivery of public sector activities (Voorberg et al. 2015) and sees citizens and service-users as integral policy actors, and 'untapped resources' whose knowledge and experience can be mobilised as 'a lever of public innovation' (Torfing et al. 2019).

References

Arnstein, S.R. (1969), 'A Ladder of Citizen Participation', *Journal of the American Institute of Planners*, vol. 35, no. 4, July 1, pp 216–24.

Benefacts (2018), *Analysis 2018*. Available at: https://analysis2018. benefacts.ie/report/thirdsector

Chaney, P. (2020), 'The Potential of Civil Society to Bring About Social Change'. Available at http://www.transformingsociety.co.uk/2020/10/21/ the-potential-of-civil-society-to-bring-about-social-change/?utm_ source=listserv&utm_medium=email&utm_campaign=social-policy-CSSC-listserv-Oct-2020

Connaughton, B. (2021), 'Committees and the Legislature', in Hogan, J., and Murphy, M.P. (eds), *Policy Analysis in Ireland*, Bristol: Policy Press.

Cullen, P. (2021), 'Gender Expertise and Policy Analysis', in Hogan, J., and Murphy, M.P. (eds), *Policy Analysis in Ireland*, Bristol: Policy Press.

Department of Rural and Community Development (2019), *Sustainable, Inclusive and Empowered Communities – Five-Year Strategy to Support the Voluntary and Community Sector in Ireland 2019–2024*, Dublin: Government Publications.

Department of Social Welfare (2000), *Supporting Voluntary Activity*, Dublin: Government Publications.

Dukelow, F. (2021), 'The Evolution of Social Policy Analysis in Ireland: From a Theocentric to an Econocentric Paradigm?', in Hogan, J., and Murphy, M.P. (eds), *Policy Analysis in Ireland*, Bristol: Policy Press.

Edelman, D.J,. (2020), '2020 Edelman Trust Barometer Global Report', Daniel J. Edelman Holdings. Available at: https://www.edelman.com/ trustbarometer

Government of Ireland (2020), *Ambitions, Goals and Commitments – Roadmap for Social Inclusion 2020–5*, Dublin: Government Publications.

Harris, C. (2021), 'Democratic Innovations and Policy Analysis: Climate Policy and Ireland's Citizens' Assembly (2016–2018)', in Hogan, J., and Murphy, M.P. (eds), *Policy Analysis in Ireland*, Bristol: Policy Press.

Harvey, B. (2012), *Changes in Employment and Services in the Voluntary and Community Sector in Ireland, 2008–2012*, Dublin: ICTU.

Harvey, B. (2014), *Are We Paying for That? Government Funding & Social Justice Advocacy*, Dublin: The Advocacy Initiative.

Harvey, B. (2020), 'Our Story: Strengthening and Empowering Children, Families and Communities Through the Family Resource Centre Programme', Dublin: Family Resource Centre National Forum.

Healy, J., and Clarke, M. (2020), 'Implementing Choice-Based Models of Social Service: The Importance of Involving People who Use Services in Reform Processes', *Administration*, vol. 68, no. 4, pp 181–99. Available at doi: 10.2478/admin-2020-0030

Heclo, H. (1974), *Modern Social Policies in Britain and Sweden: From Relief to Income Maintenance*, New Haven, CT: Yale University Press.

Keane, C., Callan, T., Savage, M., Walsh, J.R., and Colgan, B. (2015), *Distributional Impact of Tax, Welfare and Public Pay Policies – Budget 2015 and Budgets 2009–2015*, Dublin: Economic and Social Research Institute (ESRI).

Larragy, J. (2014), *Asymmetric Engagement: The Community and Voluntary Pillar in Irish Social Partnership*, Manchester: Manchester University Press.

McCarthy, D. (2021), 'Foreword', in Hogan, J., and Murphy, M.P. (eds), *Policy Analysis in Ireland*, Bristol: Policy Press.

Meade, R. (2005), 'We Hate it Here, Please Let us Stay! Irish Social Partnership and the Community/Voluntary Sector's Conflicted Experiences of Recognition', *Critical Social Policy*, vol. 25, no. 3, pp 349–73. Available at doi:10.1177/0261018305054076

Murphy, M.P. (2002), 'Social Partnership: Is it the Only Game in Town?' *Community Development Journal*, vol. 37, no. 1, pp 80–90.

Murphy, M. (2011), 'Civil Society in the Shadow of the Irish State', *Irish Journal of Sociology*, vol. 19, no. 2, pp 170–87.

Murphy M.P. (2017), 'Maximising Available Resources: Equality and Human Rights Proofing Irish Fiscal Policy', *Administration*, vol. 65, no. 3, pp 59–80.

Murphy, M.P., and Hogan, J. (2020), 'Reflections on Post-Bailout Policy Analysis in Ireland', *Administration*, vol, 68, no. 4, pp 145–60.

Murphy, M.P, and O'Connor, O. (2021), 'Civil Society Organisations and Policy Analysis: Resilience in the Context of Shifting Political Opportunity Structures?', in Hogan, J., and Murphy, M.P. (eds) *Policy Analysis in Ireland*, Bristol: Policy Press.

O'Donnell, R. (2021), 'The Social Partners and the NESC: From Tripartite Dialogue via Common Knowledge Events to Network Knowledge', in Hogan, J., and Murphy, M.P. (eds), *Policy Analysis in Ireland*, Bristol: Policy Press.

Rees Jones, I., Woods, M. and Chaney, P. (2020), *Civil Society and Social Change*, Bristol: Policy Press.

Ruane, F. (2021), 'Introducing Evidence into Policy Making in Ireland', in Hogan, J., and Murphy, M.P. (eds), *Policy Analysis in Ireland*, Bristol: Policy Press.

Sabel, C. (2020), 'Governance and Wicked Problems: Environment, Climate, Human Services and Quality Jobs', paper prepared for the Knowledge and Policy: Confronting Governance Challenges in the New Decade Conference, January, Dublin: NESC/MU.

Timms, H., and Heimens, J. (2018), *New Power: How Its Changing the 21st Century and Why You Need to Know*, London: Pan Macmillan.

Torfing, J., Sørensen, E., and Røiseland, A. (2019), 'Transforming the Public Sector into an Arena for Co-creation: Barriers, Drivers, Benefits, and Ways Forward', *Administration & Society*, vol. 51, no. 5, pp 795–825.

Visser, A. (2019), 'Ireland Emerging from the Crisis', in Harvey, B. (ed.), *Report on the State of Civil Society in the EU and Russia*, Berlin: EU–Russia Civil Society Forum.

Voorberg, W.H., Bekkers, V.J., and Tummers, L.G. (2015), 'A Systematic Review of Co-creation and Co-production: Embarking on the Social Innovation Journey', *Public Management Review*, vol. 17, no. 9, pp 1333–57.

Walsh, Kathy et al. (2013), *In Other Words: Policy Makers' Perceptions of Social Justice Advocacy*, Dublin: The Advocacy Initiative.

CHAPTER 8

Strengthening the Culture of the 'Fifth Estate'

Eddie Molloy

The public service – The Fifth Estate

In January 2014, a consultation paper on strengthening civil service accountability and performance posed a fundamental question:

> How far should public servants rely on their professionalism and sense of personal morality or should they simply follow instructions from their political masters? (Government Reform Unit 2014)

Conscientious resolution of this dilemma is key to good governance of the State's affairs. Consistent, principled conduct, decision-making and communication by public servants defines what Maurice Hayes called an effective 'Fifth Estate'.

In his NUIG speech in 2013 (Hayes 2013), the eminent former public servant characterised the civil service as the Fifth Estate and, as such, a 'distinctive, indispensable institution that performs a vital balancing role in the machinery of a functioning democracy'. The Fifth Estate must be capable of acting as a 'brake on autocracy and as a bulwark against mad and bad politics.' Vital elements of the Fifth Estate had malfunctioned leading up to the financial crash of 2008, according to Dr Hayes, by losing sight of the foundational values of an earlier generation of civil servants. While the focus on these matters has been principally on the behaviour of senior civil and public servants, the same essential dilemma is faced by staff at all levels. For example:

- What is a Clerical Officer (CO) to do when expected to process for payment very dubious travel expenses of a TD? In the particular case, the CO consulted an Executive Officer who said, 'Just put them through', and when the CO refused, the matter eventually went to the Secretary-General who told the CO to make the payment. The dilemma is the same at each level – whether to act on one's ethical principles or simply obey the instructions of one's boss.
- What are officials to do when they are expected to 'spin' a reply to a searching Parliamentary Question (PQ) in order to prevent embarrassing truths emerging? Judge Charleton, in his tribunal report, said of the frequent resort to spin in a section entitled 'Public Relations as a Substitute for Facts': 'This is a hideous development in Irish Public life' (Charleton 2017).
- What were officials to do when they adopted objective criteria for deciding on the location of primary-care centres and Health Minister James Reilly overruled them on the basis of his 'logistical logarithmic progressions' formula?
- What are officials to do when successive ministers for sport insist on favouring their own constituency in the disbursement of grants, against the advice of officials?
- In their submission to the consultations on accountability that resulted in the January 2014 paper, Heads of Audit (of government departments) told how civil servants are frequently faced with the choice between maintaining their own integrity and 'going along to get along'. They maintained that some of the inaction of senior civil servants leading up to the financial crisis was because 'their roles became too politicised, relationships too close and a lack of constructive challenge even behind closed doors'.

Famously, in their report on the banking crisis of 2008, Regling and Watson (2010) remarked: 'No one in authority shouted stop'. The reason no one shouted stop is that a heavy price can be paid for doing so, for speaking truth to power, for speaking up about wrongdoing or contesting decisions that public servants believe are not in the public interest.

Robert Watt, when Secretary-General of the Department of Public Expenditure and Reform (DPER), resisted calls to repeat in public his reported concerns about the escalating costs of the National Children's Hospital. His views were at odds with the official government estimates. When pressed, Mr Watt said: 'I'd probably be fired if I said anything'. Though said partly in jest, he was speaking of a reality that is understood by anyone familiar with the relationship between the political system and the public service (MacGill Summer School, 24 July 2019).

Conscientious resolution of the core dilemma should not call for individual heroism, putting one's position or career prospects at risk or inviting social sanctions like ostracisation. If there is to be a pattern of consistent adherence to ethical and professional principles, when under pressure to accede to policies and messages that place personal or party-political interest over the public good, there has to be a robust public service culture (or ethos). It has to become 'the way things are done around here when no one is looking', a common and useful definition of culture.

Building a robust public service culture

As the subtitle of the DPER 2014 paper indicates, the trigger for the consultation process was a commitment in the 2011 Programme for Government to institute far-reaching reforms to overcome the 'huge accountability gap' in our system of governance.

The Programme declared:

> We will pin down accountability for results at every level – from Ministers down – with clear consequences for success and failure. Ministers should be responsible for policy and public service managers for delivery.
>
> We will legislate for a reformulated code of laws, replacing both the Ministers and Secretaries Act and the Public Service Management Act.
>
> Restrictions on the nature and extent of evidence by civil servants to Oireachtas committees will be scrapped and replaced with new guidelines for civil servants that reflect the

reality of the authority delegated to them and their personal accountability for the way in which it is exercised.

In the aftermath of the 2008 calamity, there was a stream of official post-mortems and extensive public commentary on the causes, together with recommendations for reform. Eoin O'Malley and Muiris MacCarthaigh (2012) set out the full scale and *depth* of the reform challenge:

> That problems persist in pinpointing accountability for maladministration and other failures within government is perplexing, given that a number of initiatives have been developed precisely to improve oversight and to establish responsibility. (p. 264)

This Report concludes that:

> It would seem, however, that reforms targeting specific aspects of accountability are insufficient and that what is required is a **whole of government** [emphasis added] approach to the issue ... Legislative and organisational change will not be sufficient for this to be successful: **cultural change** [emphasis added] is also needed to give meaning to accountability at all levels of government.

Maurice Hayes called for *deep* structural and *cultural* reform. In these references, we emphasise *depth* of change required, *cultural* reform and the need for a *whole-of-government* approach.

While accountability is understandably central to many discussions of institutional culture, other values are also critically important, such as impartiality, fairness, respect for privacy and value for money. Accountability is the overarching value whereby adherence to these other values can be evaluated.

Efforts to explain recurring, 'perplexing', seemingly intractable institutional failings over the past 15 years have repeatedly cited the organisation's culture as the root cause, whether it be in An Garda Síochána, the HSE, the Central Bank and the banks, the juvenile prison, the Fianna Fáil party, the FAI or the Catholic Church, just for example.

An illuminating metaphor: The iceberg

Anthropologists, the specialists in culture, distinguish between 'values' and 'artefacts'. In management literature, culture generally refers to the content below the surface (Figure 1), the shared, deeply embedded mindsets, though both are integral to culture. We will adopt this convention for most of this chapter, and refer to the instruments above the surface as 'infrastructure'.

Figure 1: Organisation Iceberg

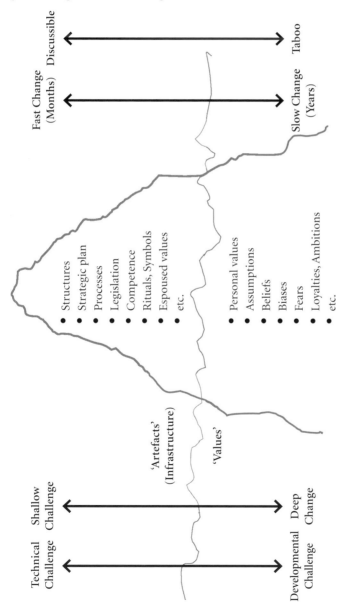

The well-known saying 'culture eats strategy for breakfast' may be extended to '...and everything else – new governance arrangements, structures, legislation, processes, standards, etc.'

When faced with the question posed at the outset, the hard choice for public servants between *espoused corporate values* (like 'transparency', 'primacy of the public interest' or 'fairness') and more deeply held *personal values* – such as loyalty to colleagues, 'my career prospects', avoiding embarrassment of the Minister or covering up their own incompetence or waste of public money, the temptation is for the latter to win out. Such self-serving responses are more or less instinctive and, when people make the choice, they will often cite 'prudence' or 'wisdom' as the rationale for compromising on the espoused values.

These overriding values are largely unarticulated or admitted. As such they constitute what Kegan and Lahey (2009) call the organisation's *immune* (to change) *system*. Hence, they need to be *called out, surfaced and rendered discussible.*

Of course, loyalty to colleagues and advancing one's own career are worthy values. The choice is not always between good and bad, and that is why conscientious resolution of these dilemmas is so challenging. Each individual instrument has a *hierarchy of values.* So does each group, community and society. Public servants face a wide range of dilemmas; for example, whether a social protection official or a garda applies the letter of the law or uses their discretion; or whether to favour secrecy and confidentiality over transparency. You can fix a problem, but the resolution of dilemmas, reconciling two legitimate aspirations, to achieve the best of both, instead of either/or, is altogether more complex.

A major obstacle to addressing this tension among competing values is that there is a *taboo* on mentioning this stuff. 'Let's not go there' is a common reaction. The very idea of questioning the integrity of people in authority or suggesting that they might sometimes forfeit their officially espoused noble values in favour of protecting a minister, advancing their own career or merely to avoid hassle is almost guaranteed to elicit an indignant reaction.

Progress on infrastructure reform

Since the 2011 Programme for Government commitment to close the 'huge accountability gap', the DPER has diligently sought to give effect to this promise with mixed success. To date, these efforts at strengthening accountability have focused on the instruments above the surface, the infrastructure.

Among the more searing commentaries on what needs to be fixed was that of Pat Rabbitte, TD, who presented a forensic analysis of our system of accountability at the Burren Law School in 2010. With reference specifically to the aforementioned Ministries and Secretaries Act, 1924, and the Public Service Management Act, 1997, which govern the relationship between ministers and senior officials, he said:

> Without statutory reform the system of accountability we pretend to operate in this country is grounded in a lie.... The current system enables Civil Servants to hide behind the skirts of Ministers and for Ministers to avoid responsibility.... If questions are asked about who actually decided what, when and why, the corporate veil descends upon the entire department. (Rabbitte 2010)

Immediately following publication of the January 2014 consultation paper (DPER 2014), the DPER continued to work with a sense of urgency on this reform agenda, with the establishment in February 2014 of an Independent Expert Panel (IEP) to reflect on the just-published paper; to consult and engage with a wide range of stakeholders; and to '...develop recommendations, including possible reform options for consideration by the Minister for Public Expenditure and Reform'.

The IEP published its recommendations four months later, in May 2014 (IEP 2014). Regrettably, the Panel failed to address adequately Mr Rabbitte's critique or additional important concerns raised in the January 2014 paper:

- On the core question posed – whether public servants should rely on their professionalism and sense of personal morality or simply follow instructions from their political masters – the IEP was silent.
- The IEP concluded that there was no need for legislative change to disentangle the respective responsibilities and accountabilities of ministers and civil servants, with the result that ministers and senior officials can still hide behind each other's skirts.
- On two other vital elements of mature governance systems, the IEP's conclusions fell short – the requirement for *external scrutiny*, and the availability of *effective sanctions*.

The DPER January 2014 paper had defined accountability thus:

> The original and long-standing core meaning of accountability and its conventional usage within the governmental system in Ireland (and other Westminster-type parliamentary democracies) is … the formal obligation to submit to a mechanism designed to achieve external scrutiny in explaining and justifying past conduct or actions with the possibility of facing consequences arising.

With regard to *external* scrutiny, the IEP recommended the establishment of an Accountability Board for the Civil Service. The membership of this Board comprises: the Taoiseach, the Tánaiste, the Minister for Public Expenditure and Reform, the Secretary-General to the Taoiseach, the Secretary-General to the DPER, one other Secretary-General, the Head of the Civil Service, and four independent external members. This 7:4 internal versus external balance can hardly be seen as a serious attempt to ensure external scrutiny.

As for effective *sanctions*, the IEP failed to meet the 2011 Programme for Government commitments to 'pin down accountability for results at every level – from ministers down – with clear consequences for success and failure.' Their recommendation was for 'stronger, more robust supports for managers dealing with non-performance and underperformance. This would assist underperformers through identification and development measures in raising their performance'. Minister Brendan Howlin endorsed this recommendation on sanctions, saying: 'We don't have a situation where we fire civil servants, but where they are demonstrably not doing their job we have to have sanctions' (*The Irish Times,* 2 January 2014).

The only consequences for poor performance mentioned by the Expert Panel are 'development measures' to improve performance. A frequently applied consequence is transfer to a well-remunerated position within the public service, in the EU or elsewhere.

On another key 2011 promise, that: 'Restrictions on the nature and extent of evidence by Civil Servants to Oireachtas Committees will be scrapped and replaced with new guidelines', the IEP was silent, other than to say that the Houses of Oireachtas Act, 2013 dealt with it – which it did not.

DPER, along with other departments, has made progress in delivering other infrastructural reforms, for example:

- Streamlining and strengthening the Performance Management and Development System (PMDS)
- Strengthening Freedom of Information legislation
- Introducing legislation in 2015 to create a new office of the Public Sector Standards Commissioner, which would have greater powers of enforcement in supervising standards in public life
- The establishment of the Senior Public Service, whose aim is to strengthen public service management and leadership across the civil service and ultimately the wider public service
- Enactment of the Protected Disclosures Act whose aim is to protect people who raise concerns about wrongdoing in the workplace
- Systems of internal and external audit and risk management, which have been progressively strengthened since publication of the report of the working group chaired by Paddy Mullarkey (2002).

These and other infrastructural reforms, that is in the instruments depicted above the water surface (Figure 1), pose a *technical* (or design) challenge. Typically, there will be a survey of 'best practice' elsewhere and wide consultation of stakeholders, resulting in the design of new structures, systems or legislation. Unfortunately, we often end up with a less-than-ideal outcome, an 'Irish solution to an Irish problem', a watered-down version of best practice. Furthermore, implementation of these reforms is often patchy. For example:

- More than a decade on from the introduction of the PMDS system and strenuous efforts by the DPER to secure its application in a mature way, regular evaluations reveal an endemic reluctance to confront poor performance;
- Standards in public office are regularly breached. Recall how TDs pressed the electronic buttons of colleagues who were absent from the Dáil chamber. Some claimed, unconvincingly, that they were in the chamber but not in their seat. Or consider the case of former Fine Gael TD, Dara Murphy, managing to hold down two jobs – one in Dáil Eireann and the other in Brussels – while collecting expenses from both, and all in full sight of everyone including the Taoiseach at the time, Leo Varadkar;
- Replies to Freedom of Information (FOI) requests on PQs in the Dáil are commonly 'spun' to avoid telling the truth, a practice denounced as 'hideous' by Judge Charleton, as already mentioned;

- The Protective Disclosures provisions do not yet provide sufficient protection to whistle-blowers. This helps to explain why the lowest score among 100 questions in the cultural audit of An Garda Síochána in 2019 were on two questions asking gardaí or civilian staff whether it was safe to speak up and whether they felt they would be treated fairly if they did. For example, for a whistle-blower to raise a complaint about poor performance, lack of accountability, incompetence, possible corruption or nepotism, a written submission has first to be sent up the management chain. In practice, many concerns will involve inappropriate actions in the upper echelons of management to whom the whistle-blower's complaints have to be submitted.
- Many of the instruments designed to strengthen accountability fail because they lack teeth; they fail to meet the standard succinctly expressed by Matthew Elderfield when he came to Ireland to clean up the system of banking regulation: 'You need invasive scrutiny and effective sanctions' (*The Irish Times*, 31 January 2014). In reality, we still don't have effective sanctions for malpractice in banking. Hence the establishment of the Irish Banking Culture Board whose mission is: 'To make banking in Ireland trustworthy again' (www. irish banking cultureboard.ie). After countless damning enquiries and regulatory enhancements, the penny has finally dropped: there will be no reform of banking without cultural reform.

Confusion in policy-making and 'ownership' of decisions

Before leaving infrastructural reforms there is one element that needs serious attention, namely the processes of strategy (or policy)-making and the wider processes of decision-making. Pat Rabbitte's criticism of the system of accountability is that it conflates the respective responsibilities and associated accountabilities of ministers and senior officials. His solution can be summarised as:

- If the Minister takes a decision personally, he or she should say so and account for it;
- If the decision is taken by the department, under a delegated power, then the relevant official should say so and account for it;
- When ministers are to blame, the system should identify that, rather than shielding them, and the same should apply for the officials.

There is a mantra to the effect that 'ministers are responsible for deciding on policy and public servants for implementation'. If only it were so clear. For decades and up to the present time, we have witnessed utter confusion regarding who knew what and when, who they told, and who made which decisions and, in consequence, who is accountable and who is liable.

In the absence of clarity about the policy-making process (that is the sequence of deliberations whereby policy is crafted), and clarity regarding who makes the decisions, we have had chaos surrounding critical incidents in policing and the justice system; cervical screening; the cancellation of the Leaving Certificate exams and the subsequent alternative student-assessment process; and the decision-making to do with the State's response to the Coronavirus pandemic.

In the absence of clear, specified processes of policy-making and decision-making and accurate recording of public servants' advice, we have witnessed forced resignations and sackings, expensive – and often inconclusive – enquires and litigation. With regard to the senior officials who lost their jobs and suffered damage to their reputations in recent times, it has been argued that these cases show that we do, indeed, have accountability with consequences. However, these premature departures were not examples of a mature system of accountability. In several, if not all, cases, the terminations were on foot of political decisions in response to public demand that 'someone has to be held responsible'.

The solution to these fraught situations is not more enquiries or litigation but clearly specified processes for making policy and taking decisions, and an accurate paper trail of advice given.

Effect of culture on reports and solutions

It is crucial to understand the interplay between infrastructural reforms and the existing culture. The existing culture – for example, antipathy towards taking personal responsibility, lack of transparency, demonisation of whistle-blowers or 'amoral localism'[1] in the distribution of public funds – has a major influence on any enquiry, as well as shaping resultant recommendations for improvement. Attempts to design 'best practice' systems, processes, legislation and other instruments are often compromised from the outset by the existing culture, most obviously in crafting the terms of reference for an

---

1   'Amoral localism' was a term used by the late eminent political scientist, Peter Mair, to describe a feature of Irish political and civil culture.

enquiry and the choice of people to carry it out, ideally a 'safe pair of hands'. Then, following the publication of long-awaited reports, the embedded culture kicks in again to frustrate implementation of proposed reforms. The culture 'eats the report'. As one seasoned observer put it, 'the mice get at it from start to finish'.

Explicit whole-of-government programme of cultural reform

The Iceberg metaphor (Figure 1) suggests that reform of any institution requires intervention above and, especially, below the surface – both infrastructural and cultural change. While a great deal of progress has been made above the surface, the benefits of these improvements, leaving aside any inherent limitations in their design, will not accrue or will not be sustained when put under pressure by countervailing values – the institution's immune system.

It is worth recalling the words of O'Malley and MacCarthaigh (2012):

> Reforms targeting specific aspects of accountability are insufficient and what is required is a whole of government approach…. Legislative and organisational change (i.e. infrastructure) will not be sufficient for this to be successful: cultural change is also needed to give meaning to accountability at all levels of government. (p. 264)

In April 2008, the OECD published the findings of its review of the Irish Public Service (OECD 2008), which had the following to say about culture:

> Achieving an integrated Public Service will require mobilising its greatest resource – its core values.
>
> Behaviour is less determined by formal sanctions and incentives (elements of infrastructure) than by values that are established in hearts and minds.
>
> Governments have found it crucial to restate traditional and new values to provide an ethical framework for staff behaviour. Countries are placing renewed emphasis on rethinking their core values in public management reform … many countries are formalising core values. (pp 119–20)

I subsequently discussed the OECD report with one of the authors and I asked why, if establishing core values in the hearts and minds of staff was crucial, they had devoted only three pages out of the report's 370 pages to the subject. He replied, 'We were discouraged from getting too deeply into the topic'. Here we see the taboo that surrounds questioning the values of public servants, as mentioned earlier.

This OECD recommendation was never followed up at 'whole of government' level. However, there are some excellent examples of programmes within specific public institutions. For example, Óglaigh na hÉireann (the Irish Defence Forces) engaged extensively in a soul-searching process to codify their values, which are Respect, Loyalty, Selflessness, Physical Courage and Moral Courage. Codifying their values led to a sustained, creative programme of breathing life into these principles across the Defence Forces. What is interesting about this particular initiative is that, whatever the expressed values of the public service as a whole (see below), it shows the benefit of tailoring expressions of values to the mission and work of a particular institution.

Another example is the Public Appointments Service (PAS), which instituted a similarly thorough process of reflection, codification and socialisation of its values. Not surprisingly, values relating to 'trust' and 'inclusion' are silhouetted more clearly in the PAS values than they might be in more generic whole-of-government expressions, given that the mission of PAS in a demographically changing Ireland is: 'To recruit a diversity of people for the public service'.

An Garda Síochána has placed cultural reform at the centre of its reform programme. A key instrument in this process is the *Code of Ethics*, developed by the Policing Authority. A sustained process of communication and engagement with the *Code* and other seminal statements of values is ongoing in An Garda Síochána. In this case, 'respect for human rights', for example, is highlighted more than it might be in other statements of values.

Whole-of-government values

The Civil Service Renewal Plan (2014) defines the values of the Civil Service as encompassing:

- A deep-rooted public service ethos of independence, integrity, impartiality, equality, fairness and respect;
- A culture of accountability, efficiency and value for money; and
- The highest standards of professionalism, leadership and rigour.

In DPER's Statement of Strategy (2016–19) (DPER 2016), the Department's statement of values re-states the above Civil Service statement and adds:

> We will:
> - Always serve the public interest;
> - Build on and develop the traditional strengths of the Civil Service – integrity, independence, impartiality, professionalism, probity and fairness;
> - Continue to commit to a culture of respect, learning and development through a positive working environment;
> - Keep accountability and transparency at the heart of our job; and
> - Treat all colleagues and customers equitably in the complex and challenging modern environment, in keeping with our Public Sector Duty.

There are two questions to be raised about these official expressions of Civil Service values. Firstly, they do not suggest the kind of thorough reflection and discernment whereby the codification of a set of values is arrived at. They appear to be merely rattled off and copied down. To bundle into one line 'independence, integrity, impartiality, equality, fairness and respect' is not indicative of prior serious deliberation. Similarly, combining 'accountability, efficiency and value for money' under one bullet-point understates the significance of each of these values.

Secondly, the OECD's admonition that the articulation of public service values should include both traditional *and new values* seems short-changed. It is for civil servants to discern 'new' values that resonate with the times we live in. But just for example, should there be more explicit reference to diversity and inclusion, to the environment, to risk management, to truthfulness or to privacy – in light of the intrusiveness of digitisation?

A further question arises in regard to a *whole-of-government programme*. There is no evidence in *People Strategy for the Civil Service, 2017–2020* (DPER 2017) of a co-ordinated programme that will ensure that the values are 'established in hearts and minds'. As indicated in Figure 1, the Iceberg, to achieve this goal is a *developmental* challenge. Any programme designed to achieve widespread 'internalisation' of values would not look like a typical technical project – with a beginning, middle and end. It will require sustained effort by committed leaders, with regular reminders and consciousness-raising events, together with periodic reporting on the health of the culture, just as other key performance and organisational health indices are tracked, for example, in the annual reports and external audits of all government departments and public institutions. Unless there is an *explicit, sustained* programme to promote the espoused values, the 'hidden curriculum' takes over; the inherited culture is transmitted to new staff via nod, wink and gesture. This informal transmission of culture explains the erosion of the foundational, traditional public service values lamented by Maurice Hayes. Culture needs continuous nurturing.

The Canadian Civil Service provides a very good example of the work that needs to be done to deliver a whole-of-government approach to creating a culture that expresses in day-to-day behaviour and decisions espoused values of accountability, fairness, integrity or whatever the code says. Unless espoused values are systematically embedded in hearts and minds, they remain a mere ornament that appears on posters or in statements of strategy.

Clash of cultures – politics v. public service

Although many violations of espoused public service values, such as transparency, have more to do with personal protection or ambition, and little to do with pressure from their 'political masters', the core dilemma highlighted in this chapter arises primarily because at the heart of our system of governance, at the interface between senior public servants, on the one hand, and government ministers and TDs, on the other, there is a clash of cultures. The hierarchy of values is different in each domain – politics and public service.

In *Irish Governance in Crisis*[2] (Hardiman 2012), a wide-ranging, penetrating analysis of the political, social, economic and governance crisis, O'Malley and MacCarthaigh stress that

> …a well-functioning public service is an integral part of a strong democratic culture…. The public service, however, should not be seen as simply passively discharging the policies of the government of the day. The impartiality and political neutrality of the public service play a key role in building and maintaining widespread social truth. (pp 222–3)

---

2   This book is essential reading for anyone interested in reform of Ireland's systems of governance.

The difficulty faced by public servants in standing up for the ideals of the Fifth Estate, according to the authors, is that the underlying hierarchy of values of their political masters is: first, the politicians own (re-)election or promotion to high office; secondly, success of their own political party; and in third place 'policy' – that is, doing what is in the public interest.

This is not to say that politicians are not concerned about value for money, transparency, impartiality, fairness or accountability. There are numerous instances of politicians apparently paying a heavy personal or political price for supporting good policy. For example, in 2009, Mary Harney, Minister for Health, supported by Taoiseach Brian Cowen, stood by the policy of nationalising cancer services, even though it meant two Fianna Fáil TDs losing the party whip when they resisted the closure of services in Sligo. Similarly, when Frank Feighan backed HSE plans to close the A&E Department in Roscommon Hospital (2011), he paid a heavy political price. Alan Dukes's principled 'Tallaght Strategy' (1987) placed the public interest over short-term party-political fortunes.

There are other examples of politicians placing policy ahead of personal or party-political advantage, but it is not the norm in our political culture. When 'push comes to shove', when they are faced with the hard choice, they normally opt for political advantage, if they think it best serves them politically.

Our political culture exhibits a distinct reluctance to embrace transparency and personal accountability. 'Amoral localism' (Peter Mair), short-termism, clientelism and 'spin' are endemic in our politics, overriding, if politically expedient, commitment to value for money, impartiality or fairness. This clash of cultures explains why civil servants frequently face 'moments of truth', having to choose between either compromising their own integrity or following the instructions of their political boss, as mentioned by the Heads of Audit submission to the DPER 2014 consultation paper. For consistent resolution of these dilemmas in favour of espoused public service values, it is vital that the work of building a robust culture continues, most especially with a whole-of-government programme to articulate both traditional and new values and ensure that these principles shape 'the way things are done around here'.

Threats to the public service

Niamh Hardiman (2012) lamented that many state institutions were 'not strong enough to resist encroachment by government parties' interests and preferences', political interests which are themselves prone to the excessive influence of powerful vested interests. Unless more fundamental reform of our political system occurs, this pressure on the public service will endure, and that is likely to be the case because: 'Although many of these features of the Irish political system have long been recognised, reform requires an incumbent government to implement changes that directly limit their range of influence' (p. 224). In the vernacular, 'turkeys don't vote for Christmas', so ultimately we have to rely on the public service to build a culture (or ethos) strong enough to contest and minimise such encroachment.

Looking elsewhere, we can see how the Fifth Estate has come under assault from the political system and vested interests. In the United States, President Donald Trump systematically hollowed out vital agencies and government departments, replacing them with sycophantic cronies, and something similar is happening in the UK – a system more closely resembling ours than that of the US. The best defence against this kind of encroachment is to continue building the technocratic and managerial competence of the public service, and most especially the culture, so that the noble values of integrity, impartiality, transparency, accountability and the primacy of the public good are consistently and robustly upheld. Just as we need a respected, independent judiciary and media, we need a strong Fifth Estate – a distinctive, indispensable institution that performs a vital balancing role in the machinery of a functioning democracy – capable of acting as a brake on autocracy and a bulwark against mad and bad politics.

References

Charleton, The Hon. Mr Justice P. (2017), 'Third interim report of the tribunal of inquiry into protected disclosures made under the Protected Disclosures Act 2014 and certain other matters', established by the Minister for Justice and Equality under the Tribunals of Inquiry (Evidence) Acts 1921 to 2004, on 17 February 2017.

Department of Public Expenditure and Reform (DPER) (2014), *Strengthening Civil Service Accountability and Performance*, Consultation Paper, January. Available at Strengthening Civil Service Accountability and Performance (scsa.ie)

Department of Public Expenditure and Reform (DPER) (2016), *Statement of Strategy 2016–2019*. Available at 051218113800-ca4247e978e94a119ad6966763efa14c.pdf (assets.gov.ie)

Department of Public Expenditure and Reform (DPER) (2017), *People Strategy for the Civil Service, 2017–2020: Developing our People; Building for the Future*, Dublin: Department of Public Expenditure and Reform.

Government Reform Unit (2014), 'Strengthening Civil Service Accountability and Performance: Consultation Paper on Programme for Government Commitments', January, Government Reform Unit, Department of Public Expenditure and Reform.

Hardiman, N. (ed.) (2012), *Irish Governance in Crisis*, Manchester: Manchester University Press.

Hayes, M. (2013), 'To Hell or to Croker', Pádraig de Brún Memorial Lecture, March, NUIG.

IEP (2014), *Report of the Independent Panel on Strengthening Civil Service Accountability and Performance*, 30 May, Dublin: Department of Public Expenditure and Reform.

Kegan, R., and Lahey, L. (2009), *Immunity to Change: How to Overcome It and Unlock the Potential in Yourself and Your Organization*, Boston, MA: Harvard Business Press.

Mullarkey, P. (2002), *Report of the Working Group on Accountability of Secretaries General and Accounting Officers*, July, Dublin: Department of Finance.

OECD (2008), *Ireland: Towards an Integrated Public Service*, OECD Public Management Reviews, 6 June, Paris: OECD.

O'Malley, E. and MacCarthaigh, M. (eds) (2012), *Governing Ireland: From Cabinet Government to Delegated Governance*, Dublin: Institute of Public Administration.

Rabbitte, P. (2010), 'Public Service Reform: Ministers Must Not Be Let Off the Hook', talk given at the Burren Law School, Co. Clare, May.

Regling, K., and Watson, M. (2010) *A Preliminary Report on the Sources of Ireland's Banking Crisis*, Dublin: Government Publications.

CHAPTER 9

The Role of Office of Ombudsman[1] in Ensuring Citizens' Rights

Emily O'Reilly[2]

Introduction

Ireland has had a national, public sector Ombudsman since 1984. In that time, the Ombudsman Office has made a substantial contribution in ensuring redress for individuals and groups who have been affected adversely, but also unfairly or improperly, by the actions of the public administration. During that same period, the Ombudsman has identified serious systemic problems and injustices within the public administration; contributed to the resolution of those problems; and, more generally, contributed significantly to higher standards in public administration to the benefit of all our citizens.

While the Ombudsman is there to serve the 'citizen' in his or her struggles with the public administration, the word 'citizen', in this context, is not to be understood in its strict legal meaning. Rather, it is used in the looser sense of those living in the State – citizens, residents, migrant workers, asylum-seekers. In fact, non-citizens in our country often have an

---

1   In this article, the term 'Ombudsman' generally refers to a public sector ombudsman acting at national level.

2   The author would like to thank Fintan Butler, her former colleague at both offices, for his invaluable assistance and contribution to this reflection.

even greater requirement for the Ombudsman's assistance than do citizens. The right to complain to the Ombudsman in Ireland applies to any 'eligible person', with no distinction made between citizens and non-citizens. This right applies also to legal persons (for example, corporate bodies) and there is no requirement that the person complaining is actually based within the State. In the case of the European Ombudsman, the founding Statute[3] explicitly provides that 'any citizen of the Union or any natural or legal person residing or having its registered office in a Member State of the Union' may complain to the Ombudsman.

The word 'ombudsman' is Swedish, meaning 'representative', and is now often taken to mean 'representative of the people'. Ireland's first Ombudsman, Michael Mills, liked to use the term 'fear an phobail' as his preferred Irish-language version of 'ombudsman', thus failing to understand the word's etymology and throwing a little – no doubt unintended – sexism into the mix. The legislators themselves use the word Ombudsman in the official Irish-language statute.

The world's first ombudsman institution was established in Sweden in 1809. It was established, perhaps surprising to us now, to strengthen the legislature's control over Sweden's relatively independent public servants. Subsequently, the institution was established in Finland (in 1919) and later in Denmark (in 1955). It was primarily the Danish model of the institution which, from the 1960s onwards, began to spread around the world – to Norway, New Zealand and Tanzania, and then to the United Kingdom (in 1967) and to France (in 1973). During the 1980s, the Ombudsman institution spread further, including to Ireland in 1984.

The former Danish Ombudsman, Hans Gammeltoft-Hansen (2005), has written about the emergence of the Ombudsman Office in Denmark. The impetus for the Office arose from the massive changes in society during the first half of the twentieth century which led to 'a massive upgrading of the legal regulation of citizens' daily lives' (p. 17). These changes meant that:

> [the] relationship between citizen and administration thus changed both quantitatively and qualitatively. It became difficult for the citizens to get their bearings in the system of rules, the political control of the administration was reduced and the established judicial control mechanisms … proved to be inadequate. (pp 17–18)

---

3   *Decision of the European Parliament on the regulations and general conditions governing the performance of the Ombudsman's duties (9 March 1994).*

When the Danish institution was established in 1955,

> …the intention was that the Ombudsman would meet the need of ordinary and under-resourced citizens for quick and easy access to a procedure allowing him or her to complain against the administration. The Ombudsman was said to be the counsel for the defence of the common man. (p. 18)

As Gammeltoft-Hansen has remarked:

> In virtually all other European countries, society has developed along the same lines as in Denmark. It has not happened at the same time, at the same speed or to the same extent in every country. Nonetheless, the trend has been the same everywhere. The relationship between citizen and administration includes more contacts than before, while the capacity of citizens and of the legislative powers to get the better of the administration has been weakened. This is presumably the main reason why the ombudsman concept has become generally recognised as a necessary control body in a modern state. (Ibid.)

While societal developments in Ireland may have been somewhat slower than in Denmark, essentially the same pressures as in Denmark began to become manifest in Ireland from the 1960s onwards.

At the global level, the International Ombudsman Institute[4] (IOI) describes the role of the Ombudsman as being 'to protect the people against violation of rights, abuse of powers, unfair decisions and maladministration'. Ombudsmen also 'play an increasingly important role in improving public administration while making the government's actions more open and its administration more accountable to the public.' To be eligible for IOI membership, an Ombudsman must, above all, be independent of government and of the administration whose actions the Ombudsman examines. Generally, such ombudsmen are legitimised by parliament – either through direct elections or through appointment by the head of state, or government by or after consultation with parliament. The latter is the case in the appointment of the Irish Ombudsman.

---

4   The International Ombudsman Institute is a global organisation for the co-operation of more than 205 independent Ombudsman institutions from more than 100 countries worldwide. Its current President is Irish Ombudsman, Peter Tyndall.

There is no necessary conflict between the objective of improving public administration, on the one hand, and the objective of providing redress for individual persons who have been treated badly by the administration, on the other hand. The initial impetus for the establishment of the Irish Ombudsman Office was very much about helping the individual person. The Irish legislation itself makes this clear insofar as it provides that the Ombudsman, having investigated an action complained of, may recommend to the public body concerned that 'measures or specified measures be taken to remedy, mitigate or alter the adverse effect of the action'.[5] However, the Irish Ombudsman also quickly took on the roles of highlighting systemic problems and of promoting good administration. As explained by the current Ombudsman, Peter Tyndall, sometimes

> it will be evident from the consideration of a complaint that the circumstances that led to the injustice are likely to affect others. Equally, there are occasions where a group of complaints, on the same issue ... indicate a common underlying problem. In these circumstances, we will look to ensure that the cause of the problem is addressed. (Office of Ombudsman Annual Report 2019, p. 7)

However, the Ombudsman is about more than ensuring redress for individual complainants and helping solve systemic problems. As I put it in an address given in 2010:

> For the last 26 years the overarching work of the Ombudsman's Office has been about nothing less than the transformation of the culture of the public service, turning it away from the inward gaze and protection of self and forcing it instead to direct that gaze towards the public and their needs. (O'Reilly 2010)

Irish Ombudsman – A little bit of history

The demand for the appointment of an Ombudsman in Ireland began to grow from the early 1960s. This demand was based on a particularly negative view of the Irish public administration, which was characterised, fairly generally, as inward-looking, self-serving and unresponsive to the

---

5   Section 6(3)(b) Ombudsman Act, 1980.

needs of ordinary people. However, it was to take more than twenty years for the Ombudsman Office to become a reality.

As early as 1962, a motion calling for the appointment of an ombudsman was carried at the Fine Gael Ard Fheis. In February 1964, writing in *The Irish Times*, Dr Garret FitzGerald was critical of an overall lethargy in Irish politics and government. He bemoaned the neglect of parliament and the failure of the political parties to engage in policy development, and made the gloomy suggestion that 'we may gradually evolve into a State effectively governed by an alliance between the public service and the vocational interests – farmers, industrialists, trade unions etc' (*The Irish Times*, 26 February 1964). FitzGerald referred to the potential role of an Ombudsman – presumably to put manners on the public service – as part of the solution to this mess, as he saw it.

Somewhat oddly, one of the earliest detailed calls for an Irish Ombudsman came from within the public service itself. In March 1964, and perhaps aware of the comments of Dr FitzGerald, the President of the Civil Service Clerical Association spoke[6] of the 'crying need' for the appointment of an Ombudsman who would be the guardian of the public interest, a guardian against the encroachment of bureaucracy, whose very existence would safeguard the good name of bureaucracy. Ironically, when the Ombudsman Office was established, it did not take too long for another civil service association to voice its criticism of the performance of the Office.[7]

Also in 1964, the United Kingdom announced its intention to establish the Office of Parliamentary Commissioner, akin to that of Ombudsman but with the restriction that complaints could be made only through a Member of Parliament and not directly. One consequence of this arrangement was that, at least for some years, the UK Parliamentary Commissioner regarded the MPs as his primary clients, and reports of his investigations were sent to them rather than to the actual complainant.

Nevertheless, the establishment of the Office of Parliamentary Commissioner in the UK generated some momentum for the establishment of an Irish Ombudsman Office, as well as an encouragement to voice criticism of the Irish public service. A flavour of that criticism is evident from this *Irish Times* letter-writer of 11 December 1964:

---

6   At the Association's Annual Delegate Conference, 18 March 1964.
7   In March 1986, the Civil Service Executive Union complained to the Minister for the Public Service that the Ombudsman was following up on all valid complaints when he should have had 'enough expertise' to eliminate cases where the complainant clearly did not 'have a genuine complaint'.

Some Departments of State with a ruthlessness and autocracy more appropriate to totalitarian regimes pronounce decisions having no basis whatever in morality or plain commonsense. [There] is no hope whatever of a modicum of fair play where individual cases are dismissed without recourse to [conciliation or mediation].

In fact, the Ombudsman topic gained such traction at that point that it attracted the attention of Myles na Gopaleen (AKA Flann O'Brien/Brian Ó Nualláin) in his Cruiskeen Lawn column in *The Irish Times* of 3 February 1965. Myles, who had been a senior civil servant (of sorts) in real life, professed to be upset at the opposition of UK civil servants to the introduction of the Ombudsman in that jurisdiction. He mused on the possibility of overcoming this hostility by the appointment of an 'ombudswoman' rather than an 'ombudsman'. (Thirty-eight years later, in 2003, Myles's proposal was realised with my appointment as the first 'ombudswoman' in Ireland.)

In June 1969, Fine Gael promised in its Election Manifesto to 'appoint an ombudsman to investigate all complaints of injustice or maladministration at local and national level'. Later in 1969, amongst the recommendations of the Devlin Report (on the reorganisation of the public service) was that an Ombudsman/Commissioner for Administrative Justice be appointed. Fine Gael did not get into government at the 1969 General Election, but it continued to support and promote the idea of an ombudsman.[8] For example, in 1970, in the context of promoting his Just Society proposals, Fine Gael's Declan Costello recommended the appointment of an ombudsman.

However, there was no political consensus in favour of appointing an ombudsman at this stage. Many elected local authority members were opposed to having an ombudsman on the basis that they (councillors) already fulfilled the function very adequately.[9] This was a position shared by the then Fianna Fáil Taoiseach, Jack Lynch, who saw no need for an ombudsman given the existing army of TDs, senators and councillors already serving the public. Lynch's position drew a scathing response from Fine Gael's John Kelly who saw it as preserving 'the degrading dependence of simple people' on 'benevolent intervention' by politicians in order to obtain their rights (Kelly 1972).

---

8   Leading Fine Gael politicians such as John Kelly and Garret FitzGerald frequently voiced support for an ombudsman.

9   For example, this was the position adopted at the AGM of the Association of Municipal Authorities in September 1971.

Lynch was accused of inconsistency in as much as he had argued in favour of the appointment of an ombudsman in Northern Ireland while rejecting the need for one in the Republic of Ireland. In July 1969, an ombudsman – actually the UK's Parliamentary Commissioner – was appointed in Northern Ireland as part of a package of measures intended to defuse the political turmoil there, which had intensified from 1967 onwards with the emergence of the civil rights movement.

While the appointment of the Parliamentary Commissioner was not a panacea for the political ills north of the Border, it did provide ammunition for some Unionist politicians to embarrass the Lynch Government. In particular, the Unionist Minister of State, John Taylor (now Lord Kilclooney), on a number of occasions[10] drew attention to the fact that there was an ombudsman in his jurisdiction but none south of the Border.

In March 1973, a Fine Gael/Labour Coalition Government came to power. While each of the Coalition parties had favoured the establishment of an Ombudsman Office, progress on the issue was slow. In May 1975, Dáil Éireann passed a motion that it 'favours the appointment of an Ombudsman'. In December 1975, the Government announced the setting up of an Informal All-Party Oireachtas Committee to define the functions and responsibilities of the proposed Ombudsman Office. Contrary to the practice with most other national ombudsmen, the Government had already decided that the Irish Ombudsman did not need to be a lawyer; what was needed was 'integrity, independence and a person who was respected'. The Informal Committee did not report until May 1977, just days before the dissolution of the Dáil and the calling of a General Election – which the Coalition parties lost.

In January 1978, the new Fianna Fáil Government launched a public consultation on how it should proceed in light of the recommendations of the Informal Committee. In November 1979, and in the absence of a Bill emerging from the Government side, Fine Gael brought its own Bill before the Dáil in Private Members' Time. While this Bill inevitably failed, the Government did bring forward its own Bill, which was enacted as the Ombudsman Act, 1980. But the first Ombudsman (Michael Mills) was not appointed until January 1984.

---

10 For example, speaking in Dublin, 30 April 1971 (*The Irish Times*, 1 May 1971, reporting on an address by John Taylor to the pupils of Terenure College and Wesley College at a meeting organised by the Irish Association). See also *The Irish Times*, 18 August 1971, for similar comments by John Taylor.

Irish Ombudsman legislation

Any assessment of the Ombudsman Act, 1980 (and its subsequent amendments) must conclude that, generally speaking, it has worked very well. The Ombudsman has the status, the independence and the public respect that are essential in a situation where the Ombudsman does not make legally binding decisions. In almost every case, in the period since 1984, Ombudsman recommendations have been accepted and implemented.

The Irish legislation allows for direct access by the complainant to the Ombudsman – unlike the UK model with the so-called 'MP filter'. However, one provision in the 1980 Act generated controversy and suspicion at the outset. This is a provision[11] under which a Minister of the Government may direct the Ombudsman not to investigate, or to discontinue an investigation already underway, into a specified action. There were fears that this provision would have a chilling effect on the Ombudsman operations.

In the 1980 Dáil debate on the Bill, John Kelly (Fine Gael) coined the term 'ombudsmouse' to characterise the likely impact of the provision. Perhaps Kelly was aware of the position of the first French Ombudsman (known as the Médiateur) who in 1974, after just ten months in office, admitted that his role was weak, and that his office was 'reduced to a kind of rather ineffectual wall of lamentations'.[12] Fortunately, the Irish Ombudsman could never be characterised as an 'ombudsmouse' and the Office has never been reduced to being an 'ineffectual wall of lamentations'. In fact, no government minister has ever invoked the provision in question. Perhaps this is because any such direction must be given to the Ombudsman in writing and the Minister must state, in full and in writing, the reasons for it. Furthermore, if such a direction were issued, the Ombudsman would be obliged in the Annual Report for that year to inform the Houses of the Oireachtas of the direction, as well as include in the Report a copy of the written direction, including the reasons for it as stated by the Minister.

There are, however, some very important parts of the public administration which were specifically excluded from the jurisdiction of the Ombudsman. Anything to do with immigration, asylum, naturalisation, prisons and An Garda Síochána is excluded. These exclusions are the more remarkable for the fact that they concern areas of public administration which are

---

11 Section 5(3) of the Ombudsman Act, 1980.
12 The first Médiateur was M. Antoine Pinay, appointed to the position at the age of 81 years. He was a former Prime Minister and Minister for Finance in France. See *The Irish Times*, 9 January 1974.

central to the jurisdictions of almost all public service ombudsmen in the western world.

In particular, Ireland is almost unique in having the State's key interactions with asylum-seekers excluded from the Ombudsman's remit. While these exclusions have always been problematic, the problem became particularly acute from 2000 onwards with the introduction of the reception system for asylum-seekers known as Direct Provision. The difficulties and inadequacies associated with Direct Provision are well known, and indeed have been obvious since its inception. Nevertheless, for the first seventeen years of its existence, asylum-seekers in Direct Provision were unable to complain to the Ombudsman.

With effect from April 2017, the Department of Justice accepted that the exclusion in the legislation relating to immigrants and asylum-seekers did not prevent the Ombudsman from accepting complaints from residents in Direct Provision centres. Accordingly, since April 2017, the Ombudsman has been dealing with complaints in this area, and mainly relating to issues around the management of the centres, such as standards of accommodation, meals, transfer requests, cleaning, and facilities generally. The substantive issues of delays in decision-making and the conduct of the asylum process remain outside the Ombudsman's jurisdiction.

Interestingly, some senior Fine Gael politicians, prior to the enactment of the Ombudsman Act, 1980, had argued for the inclusion within the Ombudsman's jurisdiction of those 'justice' areas mentioned above. In 1976, Garret FitzGerald, then Minister for Foreign Affairs, proposed that it should be left to the Ombudsman to decide which areas of government required investigation (FitzGerald 1976). And in October 1978, John Kelly TD proposed that the Ombudsman would handle complaints about the prisons and policing (Kelly 1978).[13] At the time of writing, it seems probable that the Ombudsman's jurisdiction will be extended at some point in the future to include aspects of the prison service.

Complaints to Ombudsman

Complaints to the Irish Ombudsman inevitably relate to the main points of direct and tangible contact between ordinary people and the public bodies concerned. Since 1984, the areas of social welfare, health services, housing and agricultural grants have featured consistently in the Ombudsman's Annual Reports.

---

13 A separate Garda Síochána Ombudsman Commission was established in 2007.

The complaint mix is quite different in the case of the European Ombudsman, who deals with complaints against the institutions and agencies of the European Union: Commission, Council, Parliament, European Central Bank, and agencies (such as the European Medicines Agency and the European Personnel Selection Office). The interaction of EU citizens and residents with the EU institutions and agencies necessarily differs from interaction with public bodies in the individual Member State which provide everyday services to the public. Accordingly, a higher proportion of complaints to the European Ombudsman concern matters of more general concern – transparency, conflicts of interest, integrity in public office, public procurement, environmental issues – than would be the case with a national Ombudsman. In addition, the European Ombudsman makes extensive use of 'own initiative' inquiries and investigations in the interests of promoting improved administration.

Nevertheless, whether it is at local, national or EU level, there may be a shared tendency within public administrations to keep their publics at a distance. The first European Ombudsman, Jacob Söderman (previously Finland's National Ombudsman), commented in 1996, after his first year in office:

> I sometimes feel that there is a dinosaur in every public body. It lives in the basement and guards the files. These beasts have an aversion to open doors and daylight, and feel strongly that documents should be kept securely locked away.[14]

The job of the Ombudsman is to ensure that the light does get into the basement.

From today's perspective, some of the early complaint issues to emerge for the Irish Ombudsman may seem almost bizarre. One of the earliest of these concerned disputes with Telecom Éireann about telephone charges. Thousands of telephone subscribers believed that they were being overcharged by Telecom. But in the absence of meters in their homes to measure usage, and in the absence of the provision of itemised bills by Telecom, they could not prove that they were being overcharged. Telecom did not accept that its metering system could be faulty and simply maintained the bills as issued. People who did not pay up would simply have the service terminated. In 1985, the Ombudsman received 1,419 complaints (out of a

---

14 As quoted by Anita Gradin and Randveig Jacobsson, 'Safeguarding the Rights of European Citizens: The European Commission Working with the European Ombudsman' in *The European Ombudsman – Origins, Establishment, Evolution*, Luxembourg, 2005.

total of 5,277 complaints) about disputed telephone bills. In 1986, that figure increased to 1,890 (a third of all complaints) and this pattern continued for the next few years. In hundreds of cases, the Ombudsman recommended refunds for the complainant. Complaints in this area declined significantly from 2000 onwards, when Telecom eventually introduced itemised billing.

Also from the outset, the Ombudsman engaged with systemic problems and injustices in the social welfare system. These included: the right to equal treatment as between men and women in terms of social welfare entitlements (including the right of men to payments as deserted spouses or widowers); interest on delayed social welfare payments; payment of arrears on late claims for contributory pensions and, indeed, many others.

A particular case was the injustice arising from the so-called 'averaging' rule which had the effect of excluding many people from entitlement to the contributory old-age pension. This was a complex matter but, in essence, the problem was that many employees during the period 1953 to 1974, through no fault of their own, were in and out of the social insurance system;[15] but for the purposes of pension entitlement, the period over which their social insurance was averaged ran from 1953. If such a person had first become insurable in 1974 or thereafter, the average would run from the later date, and entitlement would be more easily established. As Ombudsman Michael Mills put it in his first Annual Report (1984): 'There is an inherent inequity in any system which treats those who have paid fewer contributions more favourably than those who have paid more.' This problem was eventually resolved after the Ombudsman had highlighted it over a number of years.

More recently, the current Ombudsman has been dealing with systemic problems in the practices of the Department of Employment Affairs and Social Protection in relation to the recovery of overpayments to welfare recipients. Peter Tyndall was concerned that in many cases, where overpayments had arisen through no fault of the recipient, the Department had implemented a recovery procedure without any 'poverty proofing' of the recipient's circumstances, had sometimes deducted overpayments from inappropriate sources, and appeared to have inconsistent practices across the country in relation to recovery (Tyndall 2019).

Some of the Ombudsman's most significant work, extending over many years, has been in the area of hospital and nursing-home charges and in the area of entitlement to nursing-home care. One of the biggest of these issues concerned the illegal charging of medical-card holders for long-stay

---

15   During this period, people in white-collar employment ceased to be insurable when their income exceeded a specified limit.

care provided by the health boards. This practice persisted from 1976 until 2004, despite the fact that the Department of Health (as the Ombudsman discovered late in the day) had, since 1976, received repeated legal advice that the charges were illegal. The legality of these charges was raised consistently by the Ombudsman with the Department from 1988 onwards. And, in fact, the Ombudsman (both Michael Mills and Kevin Murphy) drew this issue to the attention of the Oireachtas in seven separate annual reports between 1988 and 2003.

Nevertheless, the illegal charging continued until 2004 when Minister Mary Harney finally put a stop to it. Minister Harney commissioned an enquiry from John Travers; and when the Travers Report was published in March 2005, the then Minister expressed her own amazement at what had happened:

> Over 300,000 people were charged illegally during 28 years. This was entirely wrong. They were old, they were poor, they suffered from mental illness, they had intellectual disabilities, they were physically disabled. As vulnerable people, they were especially entitled to the protection of the law and to legal clarity about their situation.... We are a society ruled by law. No-one and no organisation can dispense with or alter a law.[16]

There was considerable political and financial fall-out, over many further years, from all of this.

However, this was not the end of the matter as far as nursing-home charges were concerned. During my own period as Irish Ombudsman (2003–13), complaints in this area continued to flow in. In 2010, I published an investigation report,[17] based on more than 1,000 complaints received since 1985, into the right to nursing-home care in Ireland. The conclusion of that report was that the State, through its agencies, the Department of Health and the health boards (HSE), had failed over decades to provide people with their legal entitlement to nursing-home care.

---

16 Statement by Mary Harney TD, Minister for Health and Children, on publication of the Travers Report, 9 March 2005.

17 *Who Cares? An Investigation into the Right to Nursing Home Care in Ireland* (November 2010).

Conclusion

The Ombudsman is now a well-established player in our system of governance, and Ombudsman relations with Irish public bodies have generally been positive, co-operative and based on mutual respect. But there can (and perhaps sometimes should) be tensions in that relationship. The various investigations involving nursing-home charges proved quite contentious given the extent and duration of the maladministration in question. However, the Ombudsman must be vigilant in seeking to protect the independence and integrity of the Office and be able to resist external pressures, whether subtle or not so subtle.

There have been some instances in the period since 1984 when the Ombudsman Office has come under significant external political pressure. Perhaps the most intense period of such pressure came in 1987–8 when the Government cut the budget of the Office to such an extent that half of the investigative staff of the Office were lost. While these cuts happened in the context of public spending cuts generally, it was widely believed that the cuts to the Ombudsman Office were disproportionate and were designed to emasculate it. In late 1987, then Ombudsman Michael Mills made a special report to the Oireachtas to say that he was no longer able to fulfil his statutory duty, given the very reduced staffing levels. The dispute continued over many months, and at one point the Taoiseach (Charles Haughey) accused Michael Mills of engaging in 'public propaganda'. Mills retorted that Haughey's remarks were 'unworthy of the high office of Taoiseach'. When the Labour Party proposed a Dáil motion calling for the restoration of Ombudsman staffing levels, the Taoiseach said that he would call a General Election if the motion were carried. An election was avoided when the Government agreed to a review of the staffing requirements of the Office. This review led ultimately to the staffing levels being restored.

However, the Haughey/Mills saga did not end there. In December 1989, there was fresh trouble. The six-year term of office of the first Ombudsman was due to expire on 31 December 1989. The continued existence of the Office after that date required an affirmatory motion in the Dáil and Seanad. On 14 December 1989, *The Irish Times* reported:

> [T]he Office of the Ombudsman will cease to have statutory force and the Ombudsman, Mr Michael Mills, will be out of a job, unless the Government introduces an affirmatory motion before the Dáil rises for the Christmas recess tomorrow evening.

Only following the intervention of the Labour Party leader, Dick Spring, and the Progressive Democrats leader, Des O'Malley (then a member of the Coalition Government), did the Government put the necessary motion before the Dáil and Seanad. Separately, a motion for the reappointment of Michael Mills as Ombudsman was carried in the two Houses.

The general view at that time was that the Taoiseach intended, by default, to bring about the abolition of the Ombudsman Office, simply by failing to put the necessary motions before the Dáil and Seanad. As the historian and independent senator, John A. Murphy, put it in the Seanad at the time, this reappointment incident revealed, at worst 'skulduggery and conspiracy' and, at best, 'incompetence and discourtesy'.[18]

During my term as Irish Ombudsman, I did not experience such intense external pressure; but there were some difficult moments. Perhaps the most significant of these came in 2010, in the course of my investigation into the right to nursing-home care. Both the Department of Health and the Health Service Executive had challenged my jurisdiction to conduct the investigation. I was satisfied that there was no substance to these challenges, and proceeded with the investigation. In September 2010, the then Minister for Health, Mary Harney, wrote to me to say that she had drawn the attention of the Government to certain aspects of my draft report and that the Government supported the submissions made by her Department (which rejected the Ombudsman's right to investigate, as well as the draft findings made). The Minister said that the Government noted that it (the Government) had not been invited to comment on the draft report despite the fact that the report raised issues of 'special concern' for the Government.[19] It was clear to me that the intention of the Minister, apparently with the approval of the Government, was to deter me from completing the investigation. The legislation requires that the Ombudsman 'shall be independent in the performance of his [sic] functions'. While I was concerned at the apparent intention to interfere with this statutory independence, I was not influenced by it. Interestingly, while the Minister could have directed me to discontinue the investigation (as explained above), she chose not to do so.

Finally, one rather curious fact: it would seem that the institution of Ombudsman does not merit mention of any kind in any of the leading

---

18 Seanad Éireann 19 December 1989, as reported in *The Irish Times*, 20 December 1989.
19 This matter was dealt with in my subsequent report – *Who Cares? An Investigation into the Right to Nursing Home Care in Ireland* (November 2010).

histories of modern/contemporary Ireland.[20] This is rather surprising. The need for an Ombudsman was much discussed in the period 1960–80 and, since opening in 1984, the Ombudsman Office has had a high public profile and considerable success both in redressing individual grievances and contributing substantially to an improved public service. And quite apart from the Haughey/Mills saga of the late 1980s, there have been quite a few investigations which attracted major public and political attention. The history of the Ombudsman Office remains to be written.

References

FitzGerald, G. (1976), Speech at Council of Europe conference on the future of democracy, Strasbourg, 21 April 1976.

Gammeltoft-Hansen, H. (2005), 'The Establishment of a European Ombudsman' in *The European Ombudsman – Origins, Establishment, Evolution*, Luxembourg: Office for Official Publications of the European Communities.

Kelly, J. (1972), Speech at a conference of the Free Legal Advice Centre, 12 December 1972.

Kelly, J. (1978), Reported in *The Irish Times*, 20 October 1978.

O'Reilly, E. (2010), Address given at IPA Conference on 'Good Governance: Values and Culture or Rules and Regulations', Dublin, 9 March.

Tyndall, P. (2019), *Fair Recovery: How Complaints Helped to Improve the Department of Employment Affairs and Social Protection's Handling of Overpayments*, Dublin: Office of the Ombudsman, July.

---

20 For example, there is no mention in Ferriter, D. (2004), *The Transformation of Ireland 1900–2000*, London: Profile Books; or in Keogh, D., (2005), *Twentieth Century Ireland*, Dublin: Gill and Macmillan; or in Connolly, S.J. (1998), *The Oxford Companion to Irish History*, Oxford: Oxford University Press; or in Jackson, A. (1999*), Ireland 1798–1998*, Oxford: Blackwell Publishing.

EPILOGUE

Josephine Feehily

The woman behind the bar

When Sylda Langford was Head of the Office for Children and Youth Affairs, she was one of very few women in the top ranks of the civil service. Among that small group, three of us had been reared in family-owned pubs – a matter on which Sylda often remarked. Was there something particular about being reared in a pub which shaped us?

Because we were the local, we had a black-and-white television set shortly after Teilifís Éireann was launched. In 1963, exceptionally to my child's eyes, the seats in the bar are filled with women. The atmosphere is unusually sombre and there are tears. I am sitting on someone's lap. I cannot distinguish whether this memory is of the funeral of John F. Kennedy or that of Pope John XXIII but for some reason I think it was the former; it might not have been seemly to be in a pub for a Pope's funeral. The television also brings another memory: being allowed to bring my First-Class school pals into the bar in the afternoon to sit on high stools watching cartoons and Annie Oakley. In 1964, we moved to a more rural 'Bar and Grocery' where women customers seemed more common, but they principally came in the daytime for the messages, or after funerals.

Family-owned pubs were the norm back in the day, and that meant family-run. While there may or may not have been a locked door, there was seldom a meaningful separation between the bar and your home. The bar was your living room, and all human life was in it. That's where the television was. In our house, the kitchen became a card school for the 'senior players' every night. They were happy to teach us '45'. Poker was not allowed, it being considered that gambling for money does not mix well with drink.

As 'Bar and Groceries' go, our grocery was modest enough: food basics, stamps, newspapers, over-the-counter medicines for humans and animals, a side of salty bacon to be cut by hand, fish on Friday and – out the back – chicken feed, Calor gas and paraffin oil by the gallon if you brought your own can. It was a hive of activity of customers and deliveries, often managed in the daytime by one person. The irritation on my side of the counter was palpable when a customer looked for a half pound of sausages as he headed home at 11.30 at night.

As soon as we children could reach shelves or taps, we had jobs – and we did them! Filling shelves could be done from a noticeably young age. 'Shelving', gathering glasses, cleaning ashtrays, sweeping up, washing glasses, washing floors, and serving customers was the general progression as you got taller; before draught Guinness, as we know it today, the taps were much closer to junior hands. Compensation came in the form of a regular supply of sweets, crisps and other unhealthy treats dangerously close to hand, and as children we were spoiled rotten by customers. American tourists thought we were cute!

My mother was the licensee. While this may not have been typical nationally, in three of the four pubs in our area, the woman of the house was central to the running of the business. The fourth was owned by an old bachelor, which seemed to underline the point. There was often domestic help, but the front of house was family-run, demanded a family presence, and always took priority. Once a year, my mother donned a hat – an event generally reserved for weddings or funerals – to appear at the licensing court. She could not explain to me the reason for the hat.

Our living room – the Community Centre

People raised in bars may or may not have been raised by a village, but we were raised in the community. We didn't need to go out to meet the community or our adult neighbours – they came in. We saw their joys and sorrows, their disputes and worries. We heard all the local news, gossip and scandal, and listened to secrets – not always intended for young ears but what an education!

Conversation was never in short supply. The local and national news was read, listened to, critiqued, and debated at length. Matches were played and replayed. The GAA and soccer both had their followers, the GAA crowd considering theirs the superior code. Come election time, the candidates came around. Failure to buy a round for the house would be noted and might be remembered at the ballot box. Local sports clubs and charities came looking for money. All had to be supported in proportion, in the full knowledge that the contribution would be analysed later by the Committee and would not long remain a secret, with potential business consequences. In later years, the local seller of *An Phoblacht* brought a very tricky problem.

Tempers frayed betimes. Firm coaxing, rather than barring, was the preferred approach. Sending someone home to cool down was a common-sense response. The consequences when a member of a large extended family was barred for bad behaviour were sobering and had to be weighed against the comfort of the rest of the customers and the business reputation of an orderly house.

For those who wanted credit, the groceries could go 'into the book' from payday to payday, but never drink. We saw up close the impact of spending money on drink, which could be ill-afforded, and the consequences of abuse of drink – not always the same thing. When times were tight, like when the local factory had an extended strike in the late 1960s, and during the national building strike in 1964, the book got very full. Years later, some uncomfortable conversations were still taking place; some bills were never paid, and it was not always those you would expect.

The bank strikes (1966–76) brought a different role to the pub – cashing cheques. Tallying and minding those important bits of paper was a regular job for older children. My mother reserved her most withering comments for those who cashed a cheque and spent none of it in our house because, by her principles, loyalty was reciprocal. Some of the cheques bounced.

Reflections

While the extent of the influence of nurture in shaping people continues to be debated by experts, the influence of environment in formation of personality, behaviour and habits is acknowledged. Were there skills that publicans' daughters absorbed that prepared us in a particular way for life?

From when we could toddle, being raised in a bar immersed us in everything to do with people. Being polite and civil and keeping your customers' loyalty was understood – but not at any price. The tacit importance in a small community of not taking sides and being even-handed with customers and between the causes you supported was tempered; a soft spot for the *duine le*

Dia[1] and a harder spot for the chancer. We learned about community; about what *ar scáth na chéile*[2] really meant. We saw at first hand the impact on families when money was scarce, and the importance of trust and informal credit. We discovered not always to expect thanks!

As bartenders, we experienced praise and criticism veering occasionally into invective. As young women bartenders, we were treated to more courtesy than the men; we were also exposed to, and figured out how to cope with, sexual innuendo and sometimes worse. In business parlance, we learned customer relationship management, discretion, teamwork, resilience and patience. We had no choice. The connection between those qualities and a successful business was just understood – and, if not understood, was regularly reinforced by the boss!

So where does all that take things? An overarching reflection of mine is that we developed perspective, useful radar and an ease in the company of people. We were comfortable, in particular, in the company of men, a singular asset in the world of the civil service which I joined at the end of 1973 – just after the lifting of the marriage bar and just before the Equal Pay Act. And being surrounded by people and noise from morning to night, we learned to appreciate moments of solitude and our own company.

I recently saw a clip from a feel-good Christmas movie set in small-town USA, which went roughly along the following lines: The stereotypical hard-nosed lonely businesswoman is on a barstool, being served drinks by a young girl of maybe 10 or 11. Everyone else is at the townhall meeting called to protest against the woman's plans. Deep philosophical conversation ensues. The woman asks the young girl how she came to know so much. 'Are you kidding?' the girl replies. 'Raised in back of a bar AND access to the internet!' *Plus ça change.*

---

1   Literally 'person with God' – a person with a learning disability.
2   Living in each other's shadow.